MW01518779

DERAILED BY
HISTORY
- - - - - - -
THE ANGLO-INDIAN STORY

ALISTER RENAUX

authorHOUSE®

AuthorHouse™ UK
1663 Liberty Drive
Bloomington, IN 47403 USA
www.authorhouse.co.uk
Phone: 0800.197.4150

Cover page illustration, drawn by Elizabeth Renaux

Published by AuthorHouse 08/23/2017

ISBN: 978-1-5246-6333-9 (sc)
ISBN: 978-1-5246-6334-6 (hc)
ISBN: 978-1-5246-6332-2 (e)

Print information available on the last page.

This book is printed on acid-free paper.

For Calvin and Caitlin, who need to know where they come from so that they are more sure of where they are headed.

Dedicated to:
Norman Charles White
Joseph Eugene Renaux
Agnes Gertrude White
Flora Marjorie Renaux and
Dean D'souza

Acknowledgements

When I told Elizabeth, my wife, that I was surprised with the tenacity and rapidity - five days - that led to the writing of this book, she replied, "It has been gestating for a long time now; it needed to be delivered!"

To Elizabeth, for all the reading and suggestions - thank you very much. Thank you, also, for giving me the time to sit down at my Macbook for hours on end to get this manuscript done. Thank you, also, for all the conversations you have endured even though you do not have an iota of Anglo-India in you.

To my parents, for reading through my notes every time I sent a draft across; thank you for your suggestions, encouragement and comments that helped me even further. To Mum, thanks for all the Whatsapp conversations. To Dad, thanks for *Renaux Railways* and the illustration of *Hollywoods*.

To my brothers, Mark, Ralph and Bob - thanks for all the help and assistance, especially with the photographs.

To aunties, Mary and Rosamund - thanks for the emails and messages which sent loads of encouragement. To Hyacinth and David - thanks for the feedback from England.

To Uncle Eugene D'Cruz - thank you for years of random conversations via Facebook. Our conversations have been so mutually beneficial that you were the first person I thought of when I started writing this book. Thanks also, for the use of some of your photographs and illustrations.

To my students, thanks for giving me a year to remember. I enjoyed it so much and it encouraged me to start off on a project that has long been dear to my heart.

Alister Renaux, aka Ency Whyte

Prologue

"Bugger off!" I tentatively pulled my phone away from my ear on a rather crisp August afternoon in London after hearing that dismissive, but very Anglo-Indian expletive and wondered whether I would have reacted in the same manner had I been on the other end of the phone line. I had simply called a Southall number and uttered these words, "May I speak to Mrs Jacobs? I do believe that she is my grandmother's sister." It was upon hearing those words that the gentleman on the other end of the line gave me that rather memorable goodbye!

Given that we are in a rather dangerous day and age, where prank calls, junk mail, spam and hacking can arouse the tiniest hint of suspicion, it might have been quite normal for my first cousin once removed to have reacted to my phone call in that manner. After all, I must have been just some random Indian guy visiting London and had placed the phone call, hoping to make a fast buck! In retrospect, I do believe that my call was most definitely the proverbial bolt from the blue.

Mrs Jacobs - a nonagenarian - did eventually return my call the following day, apologising for her son's 'rude' behaviour and invited me over to their Southall home on the outskirts of London anytime that week, oblivious to the fact that our meeting would act as a catalyst that would stimulate my interest in genealogy.

I was thirty-two at the time, visiting England with my wife, Elizabeth and one-year old son, Calvin. Elizabeth's two sisters were in London and Sunderland, and we had decided to incorporate the quintessential touristy trip into our agenda with visits to those two cities, the Lake District and quite ironically - in hindsight - to take in a train trip from the North East to the North West of England all along Hadrian's Wall. I was blissfully ignorant at that time, but now, when I look back, I was actually traversing the same terrain that my ancestors lived in over three centuries ago.

When I visited Mrs Jacobs, my grandmother's sister, in Southall, I was introduced to first cousins once removed, second cousins and second cousins once removed, all of whom I was meeting for the first ever time in my life! Growing up in India, I was vaguely informed of Aunties Noreen (Mrs Jacobs) and Bina, but I hardly gave them much thought until that memorable August afternoon. My visit to Southall was followed by an equally memorable meeting with Mr Denzil Fernandez (Bina's husband), who regaled our little family with tales of Madras of a long time ago. I can still recall the sparkle in his eyes and the youthfulness in his voice as he told me of a city and country I was born in thirty-two years ago; a city and country he last saw forty years ago: his Madras, my Chennai! It was then that the germ of an idea sprouted and which, has since taken on a life of its own. However, for long, this life gestated in the womb of my mind. Now it is time to deliver it on paper for the world to adopt, if it ever will.

Auntie Noreen Jacobs, cajoling her great-grand-nephew, Calvin.

Chapter 1

What is in a Name?

"The surname is obviously French, but you are Indian? That is confusing!" These were words uttered by an American gentleman at our second meeting.

I explained my mixed heritage while watching a face whose eyes gleamed brighter and whose smile grew more incredulous with the passing of each word. He had never come across an Anglo-Indian before, or even if he had, he hadn't heard the story.

"You are not Indian. You are bloody colonial!" screamed a South African colleague when I gave him a condensed version of my family tree a few weeks ago. I had told him how a sailor on a French ship, a doctor in the Irish army, a Portuguese seafarer, and a Scottish soldier had unknowingly crossed paths many years ago to produce Alister Eugene Dominic Renaux! He wasn't incredulous at all; he seemed apoplectic as he listened to a story he later told me sounded more fiction than fact!

"Why don't you have those Indian names like Desai or Naik or Patel? This is not an Indian name," uttered an immigration officer as I was transiting through Kenya on my way back from India to Ndola, Zambia. She was holding my Indian passport in her hand as she smilingly asked a question that I found quite honest in its simplicity. After all, many in this part of eastern and sub-Saharan Africa believe that Indians are made up of Desais, Naiks and Patels, and that Gujarati is the national language of India!

"Which one of your parents is English: your mother or father?" asked a bemused in-law-to-be when I met her for the first time. Amazed, I replied, "Neither!" To say that I was quite perplexed that a fellow Indian could not fathom the Anglo-Indian identity would be an understatement.

These separate incidents, at varying stages of my adult life, have had me thinking, and as my thoughts meander through the maze of memory and the entire spectrum of speculation, I feel the need to put the Anglo-Indian experience into some sense of perspective.

The Anglo-Indian does not even gain a footnote in history, in either Indian or the rest of the world. Outside certain metropolitan pockets within India, the term is barely recognisable; hence the consternation, bewilderment and amazement whenever I explain how the empires of Europe colluded to form a community whose identity, importance and influence are hardly recognisable in the annals of history. And that is a gripe I have against our fabled historians: they have ignored the Anglo-Indian, which is why I have to retell my story every time I meet someone who takes an interest in "the un-Indianness of this Indian," as a colleague recently put it.

What is in a name? Well, this photograph has got the younger generation of D'Cruz, Fernandez, Taylors and Doyles.
All descendants of that railway colony called, Arkonam Joint Junction.

Chapter 2

Sex

I take no umbrage in my South African colleague calling me colonial, for I am, after all, the product of imperialism and colonialism. The Anglo-Indian is a product of an important era in world history, an era in which the economic, social, political and historical veneer of world history changed dramatically and drastically. It was an era which saw the growth of one of the world's first multinationals: the East India Company. And it was an era in which the modern trend of globalisation - so rampant with modern technologies - was in its embryonic stage of growth. Yet, despite all these connections to and with an age of seafaring traders, businessmen and pirates; an age when small European nations embarked on scrambling for nations much bigger, only to feed their need for greed, a greed, in itself, caused by "the best of times, the worst of times", the Anglo-Indian story is discarded by history and historians alike. And that is where I take serious umbrage.

The Anglo-Indian was a product of man's most primeval need: sex. Strange, perhaps, even blunt, but I am sure the reader will understand when my perspective of the history of my community takes more concrete shape.

Yes, Spain and Portugal, England and France, and even the Netherlands boasted of navies that ruled the seas in search of other lands whose resources would fuel an event unprecedented and unparalleled in the annals of history at that time: industrialisation. And with its strategic location smack in the middle of the Silk Route; its vast resources of minerals, spices, tropical fruit and veggies; its vast plantations and the decline of the Mughal Empire, India would soon become "the jewel in the crown" of the British Empire. It would be an excellent base for the British East India Company, which would become the doyen of global industrialisation.

So the British came, along with the French, the Portuguese, the Spanish, and to a certain extent the Dutch, all of whom they outmuscled to gain control over a country whose Muslim emperors and Hindu rajahs were losing their own powers and sought much-needed protection from each other. The British were only too ready to offer this, after allowing Portugal its own little slice of India in the form of Goa. Spain was allowed small, indefinable pockets; France was allowed to keep Pondicherry, while the East India Company set up base in Calcutta where it began the political and cultural domination of a vast nation. All of this happened in a period spanning nearly 250 years, starting with the arrival of Vasco da Gama in Calicut, India, on 20 May, 1496, and culminating in 1857. Back then, it was still the East India Company, not the British Raj.

But I have digressed. I had spoken of sex. Yes, when these nations built their forts around India - Fort William In Calcutta, Fort St George in Madras and Fort George in Mumbai, as a sign of their stronghold over the country, they set up administrative offices in key locations and had soldiers parade the length and breadth of the nation. They soon realised that their men needed some from of release, especially in a nation where temperatures soared and the dust swirled!

And this is the bit of history that makes interesting reading. The Suez Canal was yet to be built and the journey from Europe to India was lengthy, tiring and not for the fainthearted; certainly not for the fair sex of an even fairer race. So the men had travelled, pioneers in a new world, albeit without their women!

What better idea, then, than to pay their soldiers a little sum to indulge in some sexual escapades with the local women? And thus, a race was born - a mixed breed, a new hybrid called the Anglo-Indian! But, believe me, reader: that term did not apply then and it would be years before that name was put to this hybrid, mongrel race. Yes, we are not thoroughbreds, but like all good hybrids, we have our own fragrance and flavour. Like all good hybrids, we adapt better to conditions and circumstances, but that is another story for another chapter.

Chapter 3

Identity

So the race was born, but that was not the start of anyone's problems. It was actually all rosy for everyone concerned in those days. The administrators had their men in the best of conditions, the men themselves were more relieved and less frustrated, the local women were happy that their lot in life had marginally improved; and the children were quite happy as they received more privileges because of their European heritage.

So for many years, the Anglo-Indian was a privileged lot. The transition from privilege to confusion, from being part of the club to the outcasts would in itself, be defined by history and define history in turn.

The first event was the Sepoy Mutiny of 1857. History books will narrate the gory details of the rebellion that was crushed by the British forces, which only then went onto establish the British Raj in India. In fact, some people are shocked to realise that the British Raj was officially an Indian institution for a little over ninety years, even though the British presence in India was nearly four centuries old. What the custodians of human history have failed to put in writing is the role played by the Anglo-Indian during that mutiny. He sided with the British. Brilliant ploy, he thought, but that was the first step towards obtaining a visa of alienation from the indigenous peoples of the land of his birth. The identity crisis was born, but was still in the throes of its infancy.

7

The second event was equally spectacular for the day and age. It would change the social milieu of the Raj: the grand opening of the Suez Canal! Designed by the Frenchman, Ferdinand de Lesseps and opened in 1869, it became a boon to world shipping because it connected the Red Sea to the Mediterranean Sea. With travel time now greatly reduced, the canal became a boon to the fair sex of the fairer race and an eventual bane to our hybrid race.

"How?" one may ask.

With their own women able to travel more frequently, and less arduously, the British soldiers and administrators now felt little or no need to find sexual release in their local women and slowly began abandoning their families. The identity crisis had grown legs now and had begun its rampant march across our new hybrid race. But, it was not that bad yet; a certain sense of loyalty was owed to our masters, despite this blatant desertion. In retrospect and hindsight, obviously we might have had the wisdom to have known better, but the Anglo-Indian child did not despise this treatment at the hands of his father. A sense of loyalty would speak volumes for his tribe at another event of global and historical magnitude.

But before we get to this third event in history, let us digress for a while. How did the Anglo-Indian cope with this double desertion? The British no longer saw him as central to their overarching imperialist plans and the local Indians thought of him as someone who was too big for his own boots. This situation of events, therefore, led to something significant: the growth of the Anglo-Indian community.

The Anglo-Indian slowly started finding solace in his own kind, mongrels just like him, inter-marrying and finding common ground in his fellow hybrids; and thus, the individuals merged to form a well-knit, closely bound community, with a food, culture and identity that would be unique in its own right, sprouting up institutes, clubs and dances in a manner so unique that the British could not identify with him; nor the Indian!

The third event I alluded to earlier was The Great War: the war to end all wars, only that it did not! The Anglo-Indian, being loyal to his British fathers, now his masters, chose to fight for the British, in a war which the local Indians were not all that enamoured by! And this led to further alienation for the Anglo-Indian. The local Indians saw him and his tribe as puppets of their colonial masters.

Independence! The Indian independence movement spearheaded by Mohandas Karamchand Gandhi was the next catalyst in the identity crisis that now had an identity of its own. The Anglo-Indian was now in a dilemma because, try as he might to call Britain home, the British always saw him as a half-caste. Try as he might to integrate with the local indigenous states where he hailed from, the local eyed him with suspicion, not least because of his affiliation towards the British in the Sepoy Mutiny and The Great War, even for that matter, World War II, in which my paternal grandfather was a private soldier.

The Anglo-Indian had woven himself so intricately into history, but history and its august custodians did not find the stitches all that amazing. Hence, we were always a part of history, but never destined to become history. In fact, to ensure that I get my facts straight, I have been using the Macmillan Encyclopaedia 2002 edition as a reference point and at no juncture is there a note on the Anglo-Indian. Page number 53 of the voluminous tome makes reference to the Anglo-Afghan wars, the Anglo-Burmese wars, Anglo-Catholicism, the Anglo-Dutch wars, and obviously, the Anglo-Saxons, but *not* a word about the Anglo-Indian. We are, quite literally, history without a history. No wonder then, the lady at Nairobi airport seemed confused about my ethnicity with regard to my passport. No wonder then, that my American friend nodded with understanding and a new-found knowledge when I described the story behind Alister Eugene Dominic Renaux. No wonder then, Christopher Smith, my South African colleague and friend went on to say, "You have more colonial blood than I do!".

It is history's utter disregard for a community that was an essential cog in the wheels of the British Empire, and subsequently, in the mechanisms of a new Indian nation that has me upset; personally, and for my community as well. A community that isn't even considered as one beyond a few well-defined boundaries, mostly within India, and even then in a few cities.

Desccendants of Adies from Arkonam, now in Australia.
In many ways, this book is for all those Anglo-Indians who have never been to India, but whose parents and grandparents were brought up in the country. (Courtesy Eugene D'cruz)

Chapter 4

An Indian Institution

Didn't I say 'cog in the wheel of the British Empire'? Most certainly very little has been written about the role that Anglo-Indians played for Britain and India. Here again, the tenuous threads of history are weaved into the fabric of the Anglo-Indian consciousness, but once again history has deprived the Anglo-Indian of his place amongst its glittering pages.

Today, India boasts of one of the most voluminous and widespread railway networks in the world. In fact, its railway system is the heartbeat and lifeblood of this throbbing economic giant of the 21st century. The railways' role in the economic growth of my nation can never be understated, nor can we overestimate its value to our nation. And if the Indian Railways is in a position of strength it is today - to be so pivotal in the economic progress of our nation - it is mainly because of the role this hybrid called the Anglo-Indian played.

I grew up in a town called Arkonam (Anglo-Indian style) or Arakkonam if you could manage the added syllables the vernacular demanded of you! And as I write this little piece of Anglo-Indian history, the names of many railwaymen within the community roll off the tip of my tongue. Typically colonial, Adie, Besterwich, D'cruz, Gleeson, Dickson, Tennant, Moses, Johnson, Jeremiah, Rosair, Fowler, Fenwick, Marshall, Corneille, Brass, O'Brien, Fernandes, Gaughan, Magee, Scurville, White, Reneaux, and Renaux are all familiar names to me, the Anglo-Indian, but to the unsuspecting stranger, it would be alien because of history's lack of responsibility for my race and he might never equate those names with India. And that is where a great disservice has been committed by our historians.

A representative image of the names mentioned earlier. This picture consists of Anglo-Indian drivers from my grandparents' generation. L-R: Nelson Robson, Donald Johnson, Eugene D'Cruz, Vivian Magee and Cyril Reneaux.

But Indians they were - proud drivers, guards, firemen and mechanics on the Indian Railways - taking great pride in the trains they drove day or night. In fact, as I write this little personal riposte to history, I find myself subconsciously conducting a geographical survey of Haffieldpet, Arkonam as I place these names to the buildings that housed them in the railway colony I called home for nearly two decades. I remember the trellised houses, the warm smiles and the loud greetings as people passed by. They were Indian all right, their identity defined by being Anglo-Indian. Anglo-Indians that defined the Indian Railways in its heyday.

Yes, they most certainly did define this remarkable Indian institution. Today, I have taken umpteen train rides in different parts of the world simply because each one of them reminds me of the rich heritage I boast of by being an Anglo-Indian. And on every one of these rides, be it on the one from Sunderland to Maryport in England, or on the toy train in Ooty, India, or the Grand Canyon Railway, or the Tazara from Kapiri Mposhi in Zambia to Dar-es-Salaam in Tanzania, I keep telling Elizabeth, my wife, "Norman Papa and Joe Papa would have been thrilled with these journeys!" upon which she would render a rather indulgent smile.

No, despite the *Papas*, they were not my fathers; they were my grandfathers. Papa is an Anglo-Indian term that does not get tossed around slightly; while it might be Daddy or Pater or Appa or Father in different corners of the world, in Anglo-Indian territory it is an endearing and affectionate term for Grandfather, as is *Nana* for Grandmother. But that is another story for another chapter.

Today, Arkonam is a mere shadow of its former self, with many Anglo-Indian families having formed part of a diaspora that history has not acknowledged. At one time, the railway colony was a hive of activity; the railway shed always raucous with the loud and hoarse voices of drivers and mechanics, two of them being Joseph Eugene Renaux and Norman Charles White, my grandfathers, one an engine driver and the other a mechanic.

Yes, the railways was an Anglo-Indian institution and like Arkonam, little railway colonies sprouted up in places like Coimbatore, Podanur, Ooty, Guntakal, Bangalore, Jolarpet, Trichy, Villupuram, Madras and Madurai in South India. In fact, Royapuram in Madras (now Chennai) is home to India's oldest functioning railway station and the railway station building is a world heritage site. And to think, as I write this, that I spent many of my childhood Sundays visiting Royapuram so that my grandmother, Agnes, could keep in touch with her sister, Mary.

Those return journeys, always in the dark, as I placed my chin on the barred window of the train and gazed into the soulful darkness, warm in the fact that Norman Papa was by my side, are still a vivid memory. I enjoyed feeling the smoke from the engine pass by in gargantuan gasps or little wisps depending on the fireman's work at the boiler. Yes, the Anglo-Indian was definitely a cog in the wheel - for he defined the Indian Railways and made it a truly Indian institution.

An artistic impression of a railway engine he drove. By Eugene D'Cruz, an Arkonam driver now in Melbourne.

Renaux Railways, now housed in Coimbatore.

It is no wonder, then, that Robert Victor Renaux, Joe's son, and Dad to me, has, now in his retirement, put together an interesting model railway in his house in Coimbatore. It is an exciting project which keeps him busy and also brings back fond memories of his days in the railway colony. In fact, the project is held in such high regard that he built a separate room totally dedicated to his model railway, aptly called *Renaux Railways.*

Chapter 5

Another Institution

While the men were busy stoking fires, driving engines or working on them when they were in sheds for maintenance, what were their counterparts doing at home? The fairer sex of the not-so-fair race were also stoking fires.

Of another kind. They were stoking the minds, hearts and ambitions of another generation of Indians and Anglo-Indians, a generation untroubled with identity crises and any such dilemmas. The Anglo-Indian lady was not at home; she was in the classroom in schools all around India, teaching.

The Anglo-Indian teacher came to be due to one simple reason: she was reasonably fluent in English. Earlier on, I made mention of the assumption that people in eastern and sub-Saharan Africa have regarding Indians: they all know Gujarati. I say so, reader, because I want you to understand that the mother tongue of any Anglo-Indian is English. In fact, I was often ridiculed for my lack of fluency in the vernacular, and I still am, until this day, when I visit friends in India, but that shouldn't surprise you because English was the language with which I grew up. We spoke English at home, all the time, but I will leave that issue for yet another chapter. In retrospect, perhaps that was also another reason why we were also side-lined by the locals in the different states in which we lived.

This fluency in English made the Anglo-Indian woman a competent and confident enough person to take on the rigours of dealing with little children and teenagers. She also took no nonsense from others, and hence made a firm disciplinarian. And once again, as I say this, I make a geographical survey of my hometown and recall names like Mrs Gaughan, Mrs Johnson, Mrs Payne and Mrs D'Brass who were all colleagues and friends of my favourite teacher in the world, my grandmother, Agnes Gertrude White, who taught me much more than opening and closing a textbook.

In fact, dotted all over Madras, which is around 70 kms away from Arkonam, were Anglo-Indian schools, which taught not just Anglo-Indians, but children of all castes, creeds and races. The schools were run by Catholic priests, who placed immense trust in Anglo-Indian teachers, especially at the more formative years of early secondary school education. As I write this, I picture Mrs Yvonne Gomes as my English teacher in Grade 8, Mrs Nicholas as my brother's class teacher in Grade 6, Mrs Rhonda Francis as my Geography teacher in Grade 7 and Mr Neil D'couto as my Mathematics teacher in Grade 10. Yes, the Anglo-Indian teacher was part of yet another massive Indian institution: education. And like St Bede's Anglo-Indian Higher Secondary School, where I pursued my entire secondary schooling, there were many others scattered all over Chennai: St George's, St Mary's, Doveton Corrie, St Patrick's, St Thomas', Holy Angel's Convent and Church Park Convent to name a few, all beautifully graced with some of the most enthusiastic Anglo-Indian teachers one could ever find. In fact, St George's Anglo-Indian Higher Secondary School, founded in 1715 is the oldest school in the country, a school in which Denzil Fernandez had his education.

I am sure that the Western reader, whoever it be, reading this, might smile at the names of the saints and the schools on which they bestowed their respective graces, and wonder how such Catholicism became part of the Indian nation. But such is the diversity of the land of my birth; India might, in many western eyes, be regarded as a typical Hindu nation, but in reality, it is as diverse as it is becoming of the world's largest democracy.

I am Indian. I might not be fluent in the vernacular of the state in which I was born and in which I grew up. I do not even know rudimentary Hindi, the national language, but I received an education of the highest standard - because of some Anglo-Indian teachers, and because of some Tamilian teachers who had no qualms about working for an Anglo-Indian school run by Catholic priests.

If I am a teacher today, Agnes Gertrude White deserves most of the credit. I remember her teaching Mathematics to some high school students in the living room of "Hollywoods" - another story for yet another chapter - and I was enamoured by the manner in which she went about her business. Algebra was her forte, and now, when I look back, I realise how much I had learnt from her.

In fact, when I entered college, teaching became a supplementary occupation for me. I did not realise it then, but now when I look back, having a Fowler, Glesson, Reneaux and Jeremiah wait for me on my doorstep so that I could tutor them when I got back home was more gratifying than anything else I could have done back then.

I am now a teacher, teaching more subjects than I ever thought imaginable, enjoying great teaching relationships with all my students; but that would not have been possible without my Anglo-Indian grandmother, Agnes, also a teacher, and the Anglo-Indian education I received. Which is why, history now needs to record the contribution of the Anglo-Indian teacher to the history of the world's largest democracy.

The railways and education were not the only fields in which Anglo-Indians made their mark. They engineered the telegraphs, commandeered the armed forces and even played a more than laudable role in Indian sport, especially hockey. On the railways, and in the school, though, they stood out. Yet, this community does not get the credit it deserves in the annals of history; I have to orally recount my story again and again and again, simply because of history's blatant oversight.

I sincerely hope that this little book can correct that oversight by telling this story from a slightly different angle, and in print.

Chapter 6

A Truly Anglo-Indian Icon

The British brought to India - or perhaps even to all the colonies they made their own - the concept of the club, a place where gentlemen could meet for a drink and a meal, and discuss issues important to club and country. It was the prerogative of the gentlemen, with ladies sometimes visiting in the ladies room. While culture has changed with time and these clubs are quite integrated, they are a colonial concept which exists even to this day and age, in Ndola, Zambia. We have the Boating and Sailing Club, the Golf Club and a variety of other sports clubs hardly a few miles, at the most, from where I live - and write. Where am I going with all of this? Surely, I am not suggesting an Anglo-Indian club, am I?

Well, I actually am, and any Anglo-Indian reading this might let out a little smile, because he or she is sure to know where I am going with this line of thought. A red brick building, near the railway tracks, stood proudly in my childhood and I have many fond memories of the railway institute in Arkonam because like its counterparts in railway colonies all over India, the institute remains a true Anglo-Indian icon to this very day.

Excluded from the privileges of the officers' clubs and not *yet* really interested in pursuing indigenous cultures, the Anglo-Indian's community-like spirit originated within the walls of this lovely building with smooth wooden floors. It was in this building that the bulk of Anglo-Indian culture was created, nurtured and fostered. It was the place where the community came together as one.

The institute in Arkonam is now in a derelict state, but once upon a time it was the most splendid place to be in, especially during the festive season. As I pen these words, I recall the dances learnt, the games played, the races run and the friendships made within the walls of this magnificent building.

Interestingly, the earliest memory I have of being at the institute was of a fight that erupted bang in the middle of a wedding. Back then I was terrified; today I chuckle at the thought of that day. But yes, if you were Anglo-Indian, back in the day, you were most likely to have your wedding reception in the railway institute, where the entire community in the colony would be gathered, each person attired in his or her very best. So there we would all be sitting on wooden benches, waiting for the newlyweds to make their appearance followed by their bridesmaids, best men, flower girls and ring bearers. Quite the colonial thing, right?

No, not colonial, but Anglo-Indian. At the Wedding March, confetti would be enthusiastically showered on the bridal party as they passed by smiling at each member of the community, who would clap, cheer or whistle with a further spray of confetti. Then, of course, there would be the cutting of the cake, the toast by a favourite uncle, and even a prayer by the local parish priest before the boisterous revelling would begin, in the form of dancing, which I will deal with a little later.

The institute was the fulcrum that brought the community together and we all looked forward to the Christmas week that ran from the 22nd to the 28th of December, with that last date probably hosting yet another wedding. For now, let us concentrate on the institute and leave an Anglo-Indian Christmas for yet another chapter.

It was at the institute that the community gathered to elect representatives who would serve to protect and further the interests of the local association that worked under the auspices of the All India Anglo-Indian Association, a brainchild of the late Mr Frank Anthony, who was himself an educationist and whose name is associated with the Frank Anthony group of schools.

It was at the railway institute that the local band would gain prominence, playing not just for the occasional wedding, or the Christmas Dance, but also for dances throughout the calendar year.

Around the institute, children would play games of all sorts while teenagers might lounge around on its steps talking about random universal issues that teenagers all around the world would discuss. In fact, it was on the very steps of that memorable building that I had my first sip of whiskey over two decades ago! And, I am sure I am not the only Anglo-Indian to have done that. Scattered, now, in different corners of the world, I am sure there are many Anglo-Indian men who could share a similar instance.

It was the institute that housed the many board games, props and game equipment that were required if Christmas in the colony was to successfully round off another calendar year. It was here that tables, chairs and benches required for the weddings and social events were housed.

It was at the institute that many relationships were born, developed and encouraged, sometimes surreptitiously, sometimes with an encouraging nod from elderly aunts and uncles as a new group of teenagers would socialise at the many dances and balls. And because of this, it was - and should still be regarded, for posterity - as a true Anglo-Indian icon.

An artistic impression of the railway institute: courtesy Eugene D'Cruz

Chapter 7

Christmas in the Colony

Since the last chapter made not-so-subtle references to the most popular festive season in the Christian calendar, I suppose it is only natural for me to begin this chapter with recollections of an Anglo-Indian Christmas. But before I do so, it is imperative that I recall another conversation with someone else unaware of the existence of the community.

"So, you are from India, right? You worship cows and do not eat meat? Does that also mean you are Hindu?' a rather tentative student asked me when we were dealing with the thematic issues E M Forster brought up in his classic, *A Passage to India*. I pleasantly replied to the student, explaining India's immense diversity in culture, creed and community, and later on explained Anglo-Indian leanings towards religion when we read John Agard's poem, *Half-Caste*.

I agree I have digressed from the theme hinted at in this chapter's title, but it is imperative that I give the reader some idea of the Anglo-Indian's religious identity. While St Thomas did bring Christianity to India in around 4 AD, converting many Keralites to the religion, the officers of the East India Company brought their own brands of Anglicanism and Catholicism, eventually giving their half-caste sons and daughters their own religion, which is why in almost every Anglo-Indian locality like Arkonam, the church was another central venue for socialisation. And depending upon the brand of Christianity practised, there would often be either a prominent Church of South India - modelled along the lines of the Church of England - or a Catholic

Church. In some cases, however, like St Thomas Mount in Madras, you would find both! The same can be said of almost every Anglo-Indian city in India, and since Christmas was - and still is - the biggest event on the Christian calendar, Christmas in the colony was most certainly celebrated with true Anglo-Indian gusto.

Christmas was special to every single Anglo-Indian, for reasons that the rest of this chapter shall deal with and I am sure that the unsuspecting reader will only smile at the many Anglo-Indian idiosyncrasies that will emerge as a result of this narration.

Christmas preparation and planning was meticulous in every Anglo-Indian household, mine included. As early as August and September there would be visits to Moore Market - an icon in itself, clothing retailers in and around Parry's corner and other stores in and around the city of Madras in search of the right type of clothing material in particular, with the possible scouting mission for the right type of gift playing second fiddle to the silks and chiffons, especially for the ladies.

Amidst the bales of cloth, a good dose of prevarication on both sides, plenty of haggling and the usual feminine take on decision-making, a bargain would be made and the happy lady would walk out of the store with a smile on her face, but she would have hardly crossed the thresholds when the next move in this preparation and planning would now exercise her brain cells!

In different cities, it would obviously be someone different, but Christmas preparation would not be complete without transporting the aforementioned bales of silk and chiffon to a tailor who knew Anglo-Indian tastes; and for those in Arkonam, Chennai, Trichy, Villupuram and Jolarpet, there were only two establishments worthy of note: Gani's and Charms! And, dear reader, spare a thought for the establishments in question; with an entire community within the state of Tamil Nadu bearing down on these two establishments for a single dress for Christmas Mass, who could blame them for literally finishing their last order at the very last minute, when the dresses would be whisked away for the Midnight Mass only a few hours away, where the church was filled with men dressed in their best suits, while women complimented each other on their attire, before, during and after mass. Agnostic as I am now, I cannot help but smile and suggest that Christmas Eve was actually the Annual Anglo-Indian Fashion Show!

After mass, after the hugging, kissing and mutual Merry Christmas greetings, each family would walk back home, with expectant children eager to unwrap presents that "Santa would keep under the Christmas tree," while the adults looked forward to a glass of homemade wine and a slice of homemade cake. Now, that in itself, is an Anglo-Indian tradition.

As far as cake and wine go, each household had its own secret recipe; some preferred grape wine, others beetroot wine, others ginger wine, but almost every family would want to serve its own recipe of plum cake, liberally soaked with rum or brandy. At home, Mum-Mum, my maternal grandmother would meticulously oversee the preparation of ginger wine. I still have, in my possession, an earthern cask in which this wine was made and I intend to add a recipe towards the end of this book. And as I write this, fond memories of little kids licking off their nimble fingers the last of the cake batter they had tucked into before the specially labelled cake tins were sent off to the bakers. The tins were labelled specifically because families did not want the baker - often the same one - to return the wrong tins!

Then of course, no Anglo-Indian Christmas could ever be complete without cul-culs, rose-cookies and dhodhol, all delicacies that would be shared with visitors when they arrived during Christmas week. I now vividly recall fond evenings sitting in the trellised dining room of *Hollywoods* as Agnes White and Pauline Fernandez (Mum-Mum's sister) oversaw the ayah preparing these delicacies as little children got in the way little children always do: trying to pinch a freshly made piece of something or the other. I am sure any Anglo-Indian reading this is likely to have a nostalgic gleam in the eye and a small lump in the throat, for this was, most certainly, a unique experience shared by a unique community, members of whom would spend Christmas week going to each other's houses sharing cake, wine and the aforementioned treats with a good deal of laughter and banter being shared as well.

And, at the institute, that icon of my childhood and youth, the community would gather together. There would be a sports day for the children and teenagers with all the elders in attendance watching from the verandah of the institute. This would be followed by the annual *Christmas Tree Evening*, where the same children would get little trinkets, generously bought with funds from the carefully budgeted coffers of the local Anglo-Indian association. The community, like no other that I can think of, came together as one; again making it a unique entity.

Carnival Evening would follow the next day, with games like Wheel of Fortune - not the televised one - and Housie - Anglo-Indian for Tombola or Bingo, being the most popular ones. Again, as the names suggest, it was a true carnival evening for a close-knit community.

As if such celebration weren't enough, the next evening would be a Fancy Dress one, with children and youngsters dressing up in a variety of costumes as they once again proudly paraded in front of their approving elders.

Of course, there was the Christmas Dance somewhere in the midst of it all, and I will come back to that shortly. A wedding would be thrown in somewhere towards the end of the week and then we all, children and adults alike, would look forward to the last event of the week, the New Year's Ball and the burning of the old man!

Yes, there we would, as a community, gather together for a dance and as the clock struck midnight we would walk out on to the lawns of the institute and take a stuffed scarecrow that someone had prepared earlier that day and put him in the middle of a circle that all present would form before they set fire to him. And as the old man of the recently concluded year became a thing of the past, the community would raucously bring in the new year, with the loudest possible rendition of "Auld Lang Syne." What was a Scottish classic doing at simultaneous moments in Anglo-Indian institutes all across the country? I wonder what Robert Burns would have had to say if he knew that he was being immortalised in song and dance in a country and continent miles, and even centuries away! By Christmas in the Colony; by a community with its own unique identity.

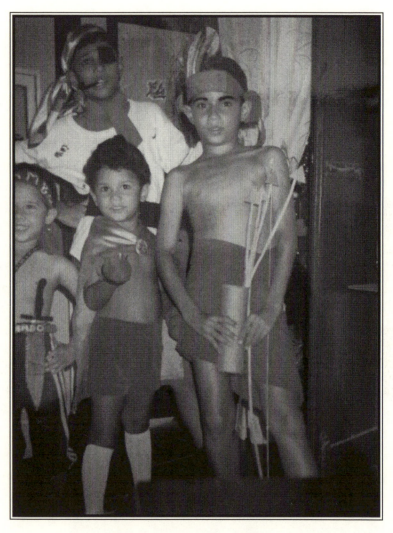

For the costume party, one christmas week
Courtesy the R V Renaux family album

Burning of the Old Man (the Old Year) to usher in the New Year.

Chapter 8

Made for Each Other

By now the reader should be well aware of the role that music played in the Anglo-Indian psyche, given my references to bands and dances, and the Grand March at every Anglo-Indian wedding. By the end of this chapter, I hope, however, to give the reader a more vivid picture of the colour and character, the action and the drama, the song and the spirit of an Anglo-Indian dance, whether it be a wedding, a Christmas Dance or a Ball to celebrate the May Queen or the June Rose, two balls that young Anglo-Indian girls looked forward to with much the same levels of enthusiasm a homecoming queen or a debutante in fashionable society would.

I grew up in a household in which it was not uncommon for Kenny Rogers, Charley Pride, Jim Reeves and a host of other country and western singers to croon through the stereo system early in the morning; or at any family gathering. Even today, I am old-fashioned with the music I listen to: not for me the din of heavy metal or the expletive-filled songs of rap. Give me a country crooner any day and I enjoy doing whatever else I am while I listen to music. In fact, *Coward of the County* and *Lucille* are songs I listen to while I cook or read or write. As a teenager, I enjoyed Bryan Adams, Michael Learns to Rock and Chris de Burgh. Western music was a part and parcel of almost every Anglo-Indian household, not because we were snobs, but particularly because of our affinity with the English language.

Being deaf in one ear, I really do not possess any musical talent, but many of my friends learnt instruments and joined existing bands or formed new ones. It was not uncommon to find a guitar or a drum set in an Anglo-Indian home. In fact, one of my close friends in college had a room in his house exclusively dedicated to his musical instruments, a place where he and his band could practise.

In Arkonam, our neighbours formed a band which is in existence to this day: The Satellites. They have passed on their heritage and musical talents to their own children and the band continues to play an integral role in the fabric of the community that still resides in Arkonam.

Having given you some indication of the song dimension of Anglo-Indian music, allow my description to waltz towards the dance that Anglo-Indians revelled in and became experts at. Going back to the Anglo-Indian wedding. At the Grand (Wedding) March, the Master of Ceremonies would lead all the guests in a promenade - around, out of and into the institute. And, while this might vary from place to place, it might inevitably be followed or be preceded by the first dance of the bride and the groom, while the band elegantly played and their lead singer crooned, "She wears my ring."

This, inevitably, would be followed by a host of couples on the dance floor who would revel in a night full of a diverse range of dance: waltz, cross step, jive, jitterbug, cha cha, and foxtrot. While the band played and blared from across the stage at one end of the institute, the dance floor was always a blur of action as couples, whether at weddings, balls or socials, would try to outdo each other as they kept in touch with the music blaring from the stage.

And it was at these affairs of song and dance that budding relationships blossomed, as young boys asked girls for their hand at a dance. I remember once being reprimanded by an elderly uncle for not escorting the young lady I was then dancing with, back to her assigned seat!

Yes, that was the Anglo-Indian manner in which I spent much of my youth; learning to live in a quaint old-fashioned manner that I carry about in my demeanour even today.

Ballroom dancing appears extinct. I have been to formal dances, here in Ndola, Zambia, where ballroom dancing is rarely seen. Dancers prefer group dancing or simply swaying to the music the DJ plays. Even in Britain, which brought the tradition into Anglo-Indian institutes, the tradition is on the wane, though one might suggest that *Strictly Come Dancing* is heralding a revival of this art form. Not so, though, within the Anglo-Indian community where the tradition is still vibrantly alive, and in fashion. Walk into any Anglo-Indian wedding anywhere in the world and you will find partner-dancing, ballroom style at its very zenith. Walk into any Anglo-Indian ball that the community might hold in Australia, Canada, the UK, or even in India and you will be surprised by the versatility, flexibility and dexterity of the dancers on the floor!

Surely, ironic then, that ballroom dancing has suffered the same fate as the Anglo-Indian; hardly worth a mention in this day and age. It is more than ironic then, that they are still made for each other.

The Satellites: Arkonam's Anglo-Indian band.
Photo courtesy Maria Renaux

Chapter 9

Don't Give Me the *Fijacks!*

English, as I mentioned earlier, was the language of communication at home and even within the community. In Tamil Nadu, growing up, I was often the object of mild ridicule because of the accent in which I spoke the vernacular, Tamil. In fact, I chose French over Tamil in secondary school because I knew I would never attain at a satisfactory grade in the latter language. There are very few Anglo-Indians I know of who can speak Tamil fluently - my mother is one of them. There are many I know who speak it atrociously - my father and his sisters fall into this category.

I bring up the issue of language because I do believe that like many sub-cultures around the world, Anglo-Indians also formed a vocabulary unique to the community, in fact, sometimes doubly unique because the lingo of an Anglo-Indian in Tamil Nadu would differ - in parts - from that of someone from Calcutta in the North East. I say so because I experienced it first hand, when I met a fellow Anglo-Indian who hails from Calcutta, nearly twenty years ago in Loyola College, Chennai. He was often flabbergasted with some of my words and phrases and even went on to say I was way too Tamil, something he said he could not understand.

I remember him giving me a strange glance when I asked a mutual friend, "So, what are we going to do today, *macha*?" Roger seemed perplexed and I had to explain to him that it wasn't our friend's nickname; rather it was a Tamil word for brother-in-law and was affectionately used between friends. Anglo-Indians would use it - and some still do - when hanging out with their friends. It is not uncommon to hear at an Anglo-Indian party, someone say, "Where is the bottle, macha?"

While the Anglo-Indians did borrow from the vernacular, they did coin certain terms that stand out for their uniqueness. One word that immediately comes to mind is "fijacks." In this day and age of Facebook, its Urban Dictionary meaning is to hijack someone's Facebook account. When I was growing up, if someone got the "fijacks," it meant that he was given a fright. Another phrase that springs to mind as I type is "I will give you one big bloody thulp!" normally said by a parent or uncle who was displeased with what you had just done and wanted to whack you, with a hard slap or any instrument that might be suitably appropriate for the task at hand. Mum would probably mean the same thing when very angry, and say, "I'll slipper you chile." And while we are still on the subject, the use of the word "bloody" was synonymous with Anglo-Indian weather; it just wasn't swearing, it was just another of those expressions that you used if the weather was foul or if the "bugger" across the street was being a 'bloody nuisance'. Like bloody, bugger was also totally inoffensive in Anglo-indian terms and tone; more friendly and heartwarming in nature.

Likewise, no other community uses the words Papa and Nana for Grandfather and Grandmother respectively. Obviously then, if you had both your grandfathers alive, you would have to call them 'Norman Papa' and 'Joe Papa'. The latter was quite interested in the state of Indian cricket and I remember him laugh out loud when a neighbour walked through the gate one Saturday morning shouting out, "Joe, that is another wicket down," which prompted an immediate reply, "So, who has kicked the bucket now, Rueben?" wanting to know which elderly member of the community had passed away!

The list is endless, but perhaps another anecdote might add some zest to the narrative. My wife is a Malayalee, from a hamlet in central Kerala, South India. When she first travelled to Zambia with me as my bride, she soon settled in quite well to the laid-back routine of life here. Almost every Sunday we would meet up for lunch with my paternal aunts who have been here for nearly three decades and she was quite surprised one Sunday afternoon to hear one of them say, "Could you please pass the *dekshi*?" Stunned, she did not pick up the requested item immediately because she had heard the word for the first time. After all, I was her first Anglo-Indian friend and she wasn't sure of what my aunt meant. It took her some time to figure out that the word meant 'dish' in English, or 'kadai' in Hindi!

And since we are on the topic of dishes, I fondly remember someone at the dining room table ask me to "Please, pass me the *doll*, Alister." No, there was no Barbie beside me at the dining table, or near me, for that matter. My aunt had actually asked me to pass the Dhal or Dal, a dish of spicy lentils! I will touch upon this topic once again when I deal with food later on in this little history of Anglo-Indian culture and heritage.

I earn my living as a teacher and I have, over the years, taught English Language and Literature at IGCSE and A Level. So, my all-time Anglo-Indian favourites are these two words: "Y'all" and "men."

"Y'all" might sound as if it came from some hoarse Texan drawl, but I can attest to the fact that I heard it from one and all, growing up. It basically meant using the personal pronoun you in the second person plural! In other words, when someone referred to a group of people as in, "Where are y'all going in this bloody awful weather?" or "What do y'all kids think you are all doing? Bugger off from here!"

"Where are we going today, men?" "Don't do that men! It gives me the fijacks." "Really men, if you do that again, men, I will give you one bloody thulp." Get the drift? Growing up, *men* was part of the vocabulary. It had nothing to do with defining the male sex; it had everything to do with the manner in which you spoke to a male friend, child or colleague. The female equivalent was 'chile'. "Think about what you are doing, chile!" would quite fluently be uttered to a girl who wanted to pursue a career beyond teaching, nursing or homemaking. And if an Anglo-Indian aunt or grandmother used the word, "blessed" she wasn't, in any way, invoking the many saints in heaven. Interestingly, the word has slight connotations of a swearword in Anglo-Indian parlance!

But, here again, dear reader, the lingo I have referred to comes from my Anglo-Indian experience, brought up in Tamil Nadu, South India. I am sure there are some North Indian terms and phrases which I have not alluded to here, not because they do not exist, but because I am totally ignorant of them as they were never ever a part of my experience growing up.

And this is what adds further interest to the Anglo-Indian story. Remember my bit about ours being a hybrid race earlier on and the flexibility it offers us? The Anglo-Indian, while one unique community, adds further uniqueness to this tale because differences in language, local customs and taste in a country as diverse as India led to a certain level of diversity within the Anglo-Indian community itself; its food, its culture and even its clothing.

Artist's impression of a house in Arkonam's railway quarters.
Once again, courtesy, Eugene D'Cruz.

Chapter 10

What is for Dinner?

I will start with the food first. While *doll* may just be another manner in which Anglo-Indians pronounced one of India's favourite and most popular lentils dish, Anglo-Indians actually do have a cuisine that is as unique as many of the issues that I have dealt with earlier in this book.

I have to start with Coconut Rice, Ball Curry and Devil's Chutney. Ever so often, my aunts, Patty and Jen, would - in the time in which they could - take us to visit my paternal great-grandmother who then lived with her daughter, my great aunt Doris in St Thomas Mount, Madras. And without a doubt, Aunty Doris would serve us Coconut Rice, Ball Curry and Devil's Chutney. That dish is synonymous with Aunty Doris even to this very day. It is an Anglo-Indian dish of rice cooked in coconut milk, meatballs cooked in a curried amalgamation of spices and a chutney made of dried red chillies and onions. I do not think that any other Anglo-Indian meal could match this one for being quintessentially Anglo-Indian.

In fact, when we visited Uncle Ted in England, his wife, Aunty Rose cooked us a meal of coconut rice and ball curry. And when we reminisced with Uncle Denzil (also in England), his daughter Hyacinth spoke fondly of the Sundays on which Aunty Bina would make ball curry and Alan (Hyacinth's brother) would run around and tell all the neighbours, "My mum is making bad word curry today!"

The next item on my menu is pepper water. There is actually an Anglo-Indian website called *pepperwater.com*. Anyway, growing up where I was, the Tamils have a dish called *Rasam*. Pepper water is the Anglo-Indian twist to Rasam, made out of either tamarind or tomatoes, with a great deal of black peppercorns floating in this mix that some would refer to as a soup. In fact, another Anglo-Indian name for it is *Mulligatawny*; another suggestion and hint to the diversity and uniqueness in this culture that is neither Indian, nor British, simply Anglo-Indian! It is a dish I love preparing and my wife and children love it, especially when they are down with a nasty flu.

A particularly pleasing childhood favourite that is presently tickling the taste buds is dumpling stew, another uniquely Anglo-Indian dish. As I write, I remember the luscious thickness of this yellow-looking stew with flat, triangular dumplings floating amongst some beef and vegetables. In some houses, though, the beef was substituted with mutton or chicken, depending on the taste buds of the household itself. I recently cooked it as a vegetarian version for friends of mine, with coconut rice and other South Indian vegetarian treats. At the end of the meal, I politely asked them which dish they enjoyed the most, upon which one of them said, "The Anglo-Indian stew!"

Anglo-Indians love good food! In fact, I remember my grandfather asking what was for dinner while he was still sitting at lunch. And I am sure that is quite typical of Anglo-Indian homes back in the day, and even today wherever they may be scattered not just in India, but across the world, thanks to the great Anglo-Indian diaspora.

Another childhood favourite is *dal mash*, which we sometimes fondly called doll smash, as children. I personally enjoyed having doll smash with pepper water, rice and fish fry. And given their proximity to the coasts of the Indian Ocean and the Bay of Bengal, it is also little wonder why many Anglo-Indians, myself included, love good seafood. Prawn vindaloo and crab curry remain delicacies I continue to savour and relish to this day.

My grandmother, Agnes, was no great cook. She was born to be a teacher (as I do believe, I was), but I must make reference here to her vermicelli porridge, something else I enjoyed early every morning, growing up. My favourite Indian breakfast is *idli, vada* and *sambar*, but it would be a great disservice on my part - and my past - if I were to ignore what vermicelli porridge means to me today. It is the tale of a woman who knew her limitations in the kitchen, but it did not prevent her from making a fast, but nourishing breakfast for her little grandchildren before she took them off to the primary school in which she was headmistress. Mum-Mum, thank you for the memories.

There are numerous other dishes of Anglo-Indian origin and influence that I have not touched upon. The ones I have mentioned hold personal memories of the two decades that I spent in *Hollywoods*, Arkonam, India, before I left the homestead to pursue my own ambitions and dreams. If I have whet the appetites of any reader, Anglo-Indian or otherwise, I will ask the reader to surf the Internet for the numerous recipes available on this social networking phenomena.

Chapter 11

Staying Back - Going Away

In the last chapter, I made reference to the diaspora. The word means, a dispersion or scattering, if one were to go back to the Greek etymology. In fact, as I began this chapter, I googled the word "diaspora," with the ubiquitous Wikipedia coming up trumps in the search. So, I read through the site and I see references to, obviously, the Jewish diaspora and then subsequent scattering of peoples, far removed from their homeland. But sadly, no mention of the Anglo-Indian diaspora, which actually did occur and which would have far-reaching consequences for many families within the community; which the reader will appreciate as this tale unfolds.

Here, the story gets a little more personal, which takes me back to the very beginning of this narrative. Remember the "I believe, Mrs Jacobs was my grandmother's sister?" Yes, post-independence and four decades beyond, even today, Anglo-Indians are separated from families due to myriad circumstances ad reasons.

I remember, clearly asking my father, a few months ago when we had a family reunion in Coimbatore, India, why Joe Renaux did not want to go away, but rather stay behind. His reply was truncated due to his granddaughter - my little girl, Caitlin - demanding his immediate attention.

However, considering the bulk of information I have since received from family - those who stayed behind in India, and those who went away to more favourable pastures within the Commonwealth, I feel I can come to some personal conclusions.

In the late 1950s and early 1960s, Flora Marjorie Renaux, nee Younger, my paternal grandmother was told by her sisters that they were looking for greener pastures and that with their husbands they were planning emigration to the UK, since they had been told that they could easily gain entry into the country with their heritage.

So, Robina Fernandez (nee Younger) and Noreen Jacobs (nee Younger), set things in motion to transport their families and young children back to the "homeland" where they would find greater acceptance than in the land of their birth. They would eventually leave India, in the early 1960s, leaving behind Flora, Barbara and brother, Malcolm. I was told, years later, that they left India because of the children, whom they felt would be marginalised in the "new India."

My grandmother, Flora, died, when I was barely four years old and memories of her are only jogged along by a few photographs with her and of her. I had some great times with my grand-aunt, Barbara and grand-uncle Malcolm, who instilled in me a love for reading that I nurture even today.

But, it was only when I met the family that went away, at the age of thirty-two when I first began to join the pieces of the interesting jigsaw in place thatI began to put my family history, and that of many similar Anglo-Indian families, in a more serious perspective. I was trying to take the jigsaw pieces of the diaspora and put the puzzle into a perspective that would make sense personally.

Joe Renaux, as I said earlier, was a driver on the Indian Railways. It was a decent job that paid well, gave him a home in that railway colony and a good education for his four children. He believed, and, this is serious conjecture on my part, that it would be folly to go away. Likewise, Norman White, my maternal grandfather who now boasted a home just metres away from the same colony, believed that Arkonam gave him all that he needed. Perhaps, that is why I became part of the family that stayed behind! My grandfathers had jobs that did not make going away a serious concern. The railways were in their blood and they revelled in the sweat and toil that the institution expected of them. No point in going away!

Remember my comments on the Anglo-Indian's problem with the vernacular? Not being able to cope with some of the office and school-related issues that accompanied this linguistic dilemma, many Anglo-Indians in my generation and those preceding and succeeding mine, decided to look for better pastures, which is why the colony in which I grew up is now a shadow of its former Anglo-Indian self.

The Anglo-Indian diaspora was a real historical event, sadly not recorded in any history book, which is why, should any census of the Anglo-Indian population be carried out worldwide, one would find masses of them - my cousins included, be it first or second cousins once removed - in the United Kingdom, Canada and Australia in particular, with diminutive populations scattered around the globe. Those countries were primarily chosen for the obvious reason that English was the lingua franca. I still do have family - parents, a brother and cousins - in India.

Yes, going away and staying behind is an essentially integral theme of the Anglo-Indian story. When I look back, it must have been heart-wrenching for Robina and Noreen to leave their siblings behind, in the hope of greener pastures for themselves and their little children. it must have been equally heart-wrenching for other families in similar circumstances, which now brings me back to that August day in London.

Chapter 12

Scattered Siblings

It wasn't my first visit to London at the time. I had travelled there in the winter of 2006 to propose to the woman who would be my wife. And with romance brewing in the air, I did not have the time to visit these relatives I had heard about as a child. But when Mum knew I would be travelling there in the summer of 2009, she made it a point that I visit Aunty Noreen, Uncle Denzil and Uncle Ted.

It was a promise I made and a promise I gladly kept, for they are an essential part of my story - this story. I met Aunty Noreen - my grandmother's sister, and her daughter Ann and Joy on one day of that British summer, for the first time in my thirty-two years. They regaled me with stories of an India they knew, an India I didn't because I had not yet been born. Ann was fifteen when she left India and told me about her visits to Madras and Arkonam with vague, but fond remembrances.

Given my apprehension after that first phone call, I decided to leave the next two visits after a trip to the North, taking in Hadrian's Wall and that trip to the Lake District. When we returned to London, I decided to visit Uncle Denzil - Robina's husband - and his daughter, Hyacinth.

It is a visit I will never forget. Denzil Fernandez spoke of his life in India, visits he enjoyed from his sister-in-law, Flora and her husband, Joe Renaux; his time growing up in Chennai; his wooing of my grandaunt and his education at St George's. He had me astounded when he recalled the names of every suburban railway station from Madras Beach to Tambaram, another suburb of Madras. I then quietly took up the courage to ask him, "Uncle Denzil, why then, did you leave?" His reply, "Unlike your Grandad Joe, my son, my prospects were diminishing! And I wanted the best for my children." I, then, did another recall on the "staying behind-going away" theme that is the undercurrent of almost every Anglo-Indian family I am familiar with.

I left Ted Scanlon for last. I remembered him vividly. Whenever he visited Arkonam, he would stay at *Hollywoods* where he and Norman Papa would recall the days of their youth. He would always send me out to get him some beer, and when I returned to the homestead with the requisite *Kingfishers*, he would always tell me to "keep the change."

His laughter, when I recalled those incidents in our first meeting after nearly 16 years, still reverberates in my ears. He showed me photographs of himself in his younger days, photographs with Norman Papa and photographs of his first days as an Anglo-Indian emigrant in the UK in the early 1970s. Once again, I ventured the question, "Why you, and not Norman Papa?" His answer, to a certain extent, had me venture another take on the diaspora. He replied, "In those days, my son, sometimes, colour also did matter." I looked into his blue eyes and his wrinkled fair skin and called to mind Norman Papa, who was the most stockily-built and swarthiest of Anglo-Indian men I have ever seen, and took another slant on my Anglo-Indian story.

In those three meetings, within the course of a month, I took an interesting perspective on the Anglo-Indian story, my story. I am sure there are Anglo-Indians in Australia, the UK and Canada who may feel the same way I did during that balmy August in England, but I am sure they may also have their own personal perspective. I hope that this story only stimulates their memories of families they met many, long years later. And I feel sad for those who have not had the opportunity to reunite with loved ones who went away or stayed behind.

Denzil Fernandez never ever got back to seeing his beloved Madras. He only got to experience a vicarious reunion with the city when his daughter, Hyacinth's husband, David, travelled there a little over four years ago and returned home with photographs of the Catholic Church perched on the top of the mount. It was the wrong church, but one can't blame David for not knowing any better. It was only after a subsequent visit with Hyacinth, that they managed to obtain photographs and video footage of the St Thomas Garrison Church where both Denzil and Robina were confirmed and married. This was a vicarious experience which Denzil Fernandez revelled in as it brought smiles to his face and tears to his eyes.

Noreen Jacobs and her cousin, May Mobsby visited India in the late 1970s and Bina was invited to join them, but declined the offer because she imagined "her India" would have changed and she wanted to remember it as she had left it in 1963. Bina would never meet Barbara ever after that and only a sad phone call was exchanged when Aunty Barbie, as we all called her, passed away in Little Mount in 1992.

Imagine, dear reader, of the angst and despair that must have been rife in Anglo-Indian homes, especially during those two decades post independence. I, for sure, can only imagine. In reality, families were slowly and sadly coming to terms with the fact that they would no longer remain close-knit families, but scattered siblings separated by seas and oceans.

L to R: Ian, not AI - Rod's adopted eldest son; Alister; Alan - Denzil's youngest son; Daniel - Alan's son; Russell - Rod's second son and Rod - Denzil's eldest son. They are, Rod and Alan, first cousins once removed; Daniel and Russell, second cousins. I met them for the first time when I was thirty two, because of Scattered Siblings.

Chapter 13

Pieces of Wood

When the Europeans came to India they brought something else which was alien to the Indians at that time: elevated furniture. In India, it was the norm in the 1600s to sit on the floor to eat and socialise. There were no chairs and tables; either nothing or a mat, a piece of cloth or cushions of various materials, depending on the affluence attached to a particular home. So, when the Portuguese first arrived they had to make do at first before employing local artisans so they could be taught how to make furniture required by the Portuguese. The same happened with the Dutch, French, Spanish and British when they arrived in succession. Of course, I have already mentioned how the British gained a major part of India, and elevated furniture came to stay. In India today, one can find examples of English, French, Portuguese, Dutch, and Spanish chairs, chests, desk, dining tables, and cupboards all made in imitation of the prevailing European influences between the 1600s and 1900s.

While many homes in India today do use elevated furniture, some of it being quite expensive, there are two items of furniture, again quite unique to the Anglo-Indian way of life, that hold special meaning to me, and probably to any Anglo-Indian reading this: the meat safe and the chest of drawers.

Tucked in the left-hand corner of our dining room, the meat-safe stood proudly, its legs nicely balanced on four square cement blocks that carried moats of water within them. The wood always smelled warm and delicious while the mesh provided a nice view of the different goodies in its three tiers of fresh warmth. I remember my brother and I taking turns to fill the moats of water around all four legs.

"Don't spill the water, now," Mum-Mum would say.

"But, why do you fill these holes with water?" I would ask, curious as usual.

"So that the ants and insects don't climb up and eat the food," Papa would say gently.

Knowledge would dawn on our faces and we'd continue eagerly. Today, as memory brings back that conversation, I can smell the dankness of the water as it filled up the moats. That is my meaning of a meat safe.

The mesh, I was later told, was not actually meant so that wide-eyed children could come back from school and gaze into the meat safe to see what goodies were in store for the night. It was meant to circulate air inside and ventilate the meat safe so that it was cool enough. It also prevented flies and other insects from flitting about those delicious treats. That is my meaning of a meat safe.

Memory now reminds me of those Sunday afternoons when all was quiet and the household would be having a little lie-down. Quietly, my brother, Mark and I, would sneak up to it and open it up to dig our hands into the jars of jaggery stored on the bottommost shelf. That was as far as we could reach back then. Often, someone else would join us on these afternoon quests: Norman Papa. More stealthily than we imagined ourselves to be, he would dig into those jars and hand over chunks of jaggery quietly whispering, "Don't tell anyone, ok?" Happy and excited to have an adult partner in crime, we would nod vigorously. That is my meaning of a meat safe.

The fridge was there, of course. I do not know when it was acquired, but I was still a very wee lad, for I remember it was on the opposite end of the meat safe. Still, for all its 'luxurious' properties the fridge could not rival the meat safe. For on top of that antiquated piece of furniture were tins: bread tins, cake tins, biscuit tins, all types of tins. The tin that received a lot of attention from yours truly was the *appalam* tin. Just before lunch, now and then, I would get a little stool and jump up to grab an appalam or two when no one was around. Getting to it was a tricky business, for if only the tin slipped out of my hands as I stood on tip-toe, there would be scattered evidence of my crime. And that is something I did not want, did I? That is my meaning of a meat safe.

As I grew older, the meat safe became a place for coffee and tea. It became a place of more modern mass-marketed crisps and cookies. It became a place from which we would serve ourselves lunch and dinner. It became a place from which I would serve my now ageing grandmother lunch, dinner and soup. Of course, trips to the fridge became more frequent and slowly, the meat safe wasn't as exciting as it used to be. Yet, it still stood there, an antiquated, but proud piece of furniture. That is my meaning of a meat safe.

The meat safe, I am sure, was definitely a part of Anglo-Indian iconography during my generation and preceding ones as well. Given the modern technology around us, though, it is close to, if not already at extinction. Whether the meat safe offered others like me some sort of meaning in their childhood, I do not know. Whether it has now become a repertory of childhood memory spontaneously recollected in adulthood, I do not know. Whether the meat safe that I have alluded to throughout this piece still exists, I do not know. Whether it has been confined to the scrap heap is also a question I cannot answer, for since I left home nearly two decades ago to forge my own life, the pressures and concerns of adulthood put that childhood love affair far away from my mind: until today. One thing I do know: it will continue to be a tangible part of my life! Why? Simply because today, it is the 'safe' of an enchanted childhood, one that I was privileged to receive from doting grandparents in quaint and quiet little Arkonam. That is my meaning of the meat safe.

Sometime in the middle of last night, I found Elizabeth, Calvin and myself sleeping in the right wing bedroom of *Hollywoods* in Arkonam. The dream was so atmospheric that I could feel it in every fibre of my being. I could smell the dark night, hear the rumble of a train in the distance, feel the cosiness of the room as the fan twirled overhead, taste the custard apples on the rustling trees just outside those windows and, most important of all, open my eyes just enough to see shadows of the furniture around the room. So content was I that I could feel the glow of the dream and longed for it to continue! As the reader should know, dreams have a tendency to come to an abrupt end and mine was no exception. Long after the visions had faded away from the drowsiness of sleep, I kept closing my eyes tighter than usual hoping to get a glimpse and feel of such nostalgic magic at least once more for the night. And therein lies the irony: in trying to fall asleep to replicate the dream of a moment ago, I stayed awake and 'dreamt' of a bedroom I shared with my grandmother for the last four years of my life in sleepy but wonderful AJJ.

And as I dreamt, faces and moments came to life. It was in that very room that Norman and Agnes White told a curious eight-year-old that babies were sent by Jesus from heaven. It was in that very room that I began a lifelong love for reading; in fact, a few years ago when I visited the JFK assassination site, that I remembered the *Warren Commission* report which I had read over a couple of warm afternoons in that room. It was in that very room that wrestling matches would be held by four cousins every summer holiday, supervised and refereed by an equally, if not more boisterous, grandfather. It was in that very room where I sat and listened to J E Renaux's stories as he lay in bed after fracturing his hip. It was in that very room one afternoon where I read an article that would create an enduring passion for travel: a Reader's Digest dissection of the Serengeti.

Thus Memory began inundating my mind by creating a collage of timelessness! Past became present and present became past. The past was even engulfed in a future it had already achieved; the future was being mapped out by a past so sure of itself. So Memory propelled me on a journey beyond time and space. One moment I was in the quiet calm of an Arkonam evening and in the next I found myself in the hectic rush of the New York minute. I found myself finishing Jeffrey Archer's *Kane and Abel* on the doorsteps of *Hollywoods* just moments before reading *Silas Marner* as trucks chugged up break-down hill in Ndola. Coconut rice and ball curry tickled the taste buds to instantly give way to black pudding on a balmy August morning in Hexham, England. I smiled ironically: Memory was giving me a globetrotting workout!

While the chest of drawers is not exclusive to any single group, it does have a rich colonial heritage and it is little wonder that it is most often associated with the British Raj. It actually evolved from campaign furniture that British officers used to transport their goods and perhaps that is why it is a sturdy, shoulder-height piece of furniture containing a range of horizontal drawers stacked one on top of the other. The British Raj and the chest of drawers developed an elective affinity for each other and by the end of the Raj, campaign furniture was evocative of the days of luxurious travel by the officers of the British army and navy. No wonder, then, that the 3 chests of drawers that graced *Hollywoods*, 76, Mosur High Road, were sturdy, smelt of old wood and, though the sheen had since gone, were graced with ornate handles that pulled the drawers out. Three quarters of them consisted of three large rectangular drawers of little more than a metre long, while the top quarter had two smaller, square drawers that could be pulled out separately.

Memory, not to be held at bay for long, demands more of my time; and I acquiesce. After all, it can only offer my personal narrative on the chest of drawers. It is rather strange that inanimate objects, by mere association alone, can stir emotions, start conversations, become part of a family's legacy and even forge one's personal identity; but such is the character of these objects which are a part of my Anglo-Indian heritage! They tell a story, weaving a narrative that defines me and my growth from boy to man.

The unknowing reader might ask: "What narrative can be told by pieces of wood put together so as to conveniently store undergarments, curtains, bedspreads, cushion covers, assortments of medical supplies and sometimes, photo albums, diaries and books?" But aren't they all little items that we use in our day-to-day lives, insignificant items that are essential to our well-being and life in general? Now and then, our associations with these obligatory articles of clothing or furniture create situations, events and conversations that linger in moments of nostalgic solitude or dominate the banter at family reunions. I am sure the reader can relate to the following lines of thought: "Remember the time you hid in the almirah and locked yourself in?" "You should have seen the look on Jack's face when we caught him with his hands in the cookie jar!" "The most hilarious of all was the time Jill's hair caught fire at the stove!"

Likewise, the chest of drawers provides me with such wonderful moments that continue to define my character. For instance, I remember helping Mum-Mum put away Papa's vests and house-shorts in those drawers. He had a uniform set of white vests and baggy grey shorts which he would always wear at home. When those vests and shorts come to mind, I vividly picture him sitting at the writing table in our "front room" in those very vests and baggy greys composing another ditty and writing another piece. The writer I am today takes inspiration from those moments in time; moments that will forever be a part of my psyche.

On top of the chest of drawers or in one of the top drawers, one would find items like brushes, combs and sometimes candle stands. Growing up with two sexagenarian grandparents, I remember standing up in front of those chests and having my hair combed just before we set off for school. The pat-pat of the powder puff still resonates against my cheeks as Mum-Mum or Papa told us umpteen stories each day as we got ready for school.

And then, there was THAT day! Naturally inquisitive, I had been harbouring suspicions about a rather burning affair for some time now. It had started around four months ago and events of the recent days had me more doubtful than ever. I had decided to investigate. Someone had hidden something of value in one of those drawers! So, on that eventful day when all the adults were having their afternoon nap, I played stealth with stealth and slowly opened one chest after another. Imagine my feelings, when I discovered what I had been looking for: elation nudged regret, consternation grappled with assurance. I had made an important discovery, for there, hidden in the recesses of the second drawer from bottom was enough evidence of my sleuthing: a green, gold and red package screamed at me, "There is no such thing as Santa Claus!" Ten years of an ideal world was slowly giving way to reality. Boyhood was changing and I had made a seminal discovery that almost all of us make at some point in our lives.

With much of the family abroad, those chests – at least the top drawers – would be loaded with albums and come holiday time, those albums would come out and stories would be told and retold, sometimes garnished with the Anglo-Indian flair for exaggeration. New photos would be taken and new albums, meticulously made, would add to an already burgeoning collection. The fact that Mr Ralph Renaux is now posting photographs taken over two decades, even three decades ago on this new-fangled digital repertory called Facebook is testament to the kind of history those chest of drawers held.

They held the history of boys who would become men and of a family that would stay together no matter how far apart they were in reality. The history of a microcosm of the Anglo-Indian story was securely maintained in those drawers. The poor Scottish shoemaker, the reputed Irish surgeon, the philandering Frenchman and the Portuguese sailor would never have realised, when they left the shores of their respective countries, that they would one day be the creators of a legacy that can today be called Anglo-Indian.

As time went on, I began to use one of the top drawers for school books and college records. For three years that drawer held evidence of a truly life-changing experience for me: my period of scholarship study at Boston College. That simple drawer held the aspirations and ambitions of a small-town boy who dared to dream big. Every time I opened that drawer for something or the other, there was this document – a sheet of my time at BC – that told me I had the character to meet my ambitions. That chest of drawers held not only where I came from, but held on to evidence that could spur me on to where I could possibly go. At one time, in fact, just before I left the shores of India for overseas occupation, one of those top drawers held together the romantic correspondence of four years!

I suppose I am, in true Anglo-Indian fashion, over-romanticising a simple piece of furniture, but in doing so I am trying to keep alive – at least in my writing – a time and place when simple things gave great pleasures. Today, Anglo-Indian railway colonies all around India are dilapidated versions of their former glories as are the many plantations, barracks and gold fields that were always filled with an Anglo-Indian aura. My efforts are to re-create – in writing poetry and prose – those good old days. In this piece, I hope I have created an atmosphere of what those chests meant to Anglo-Indian families and to make any Anglo-Indian reading this piece re-create his or her own personal history, a period of life when the legacy of colonialism was slowly fading away and the Anglo-Indian was trying to find his own place in a new India; and it is but ironic that such quirky pieces of furniture like the meatsafe, the easy chair, and the chest of drawers did, to some degree, help him maintain an identity proudly Anglo-Indian.

And, if I have been quite elaborate in my descriptions of these pieces of furniture, it is because they made *Hollywoods* home.

A meatsafe: courtesy Eleanor Rozario.

Mum-mum's chest of drawers, now in the possession of my brother, Mark.

Chapter 14

Dingo Dango

Another aspect of most Anglo-Indian homes is the prominent place that pets play in the household. Now, I am quite aware that this is not a feature that is remotely unique to the community, but I do believe it is an essential part of my story, as well as the Anglo-Indian story.

The earliest memory I have of an Anglo-Indian pet is that of being chased by the Douyere's dog, a fluffly white terrier, when I accompanied Aunty Mary on one of her visits to their house. And now, as I write, I recall the many Anglo-Indian houses with pets in the area.

I know the Fernandez' had one because the blighter bit me as I stood by the roadside and spoke to my friend, Charmayne who had him on a leash.

I remember Uncle Phillip Jeremiah having two massive dogs, a Doberman and a German Shepherd, and if memory serves me right, he also had a Great Dane somewhere along the line.

My cousin in Coimbatore, Shelley Renaux, recently turned Gambian, adores anything on four legs and devotes much of her time towards the rearing of her many pets.

Her cats were given pretty much a free reign of the house by Aunty Barbie and she enjoyed having them around her.

The Marshalls, living adjacent to us had loads of pets and it was through them that we had acquired a little puppy - as a present for Bob and Ralph on their fifth birthday. A little bundle of energy "wrapped" up for the birthday boys in a little shoebox quietly reared his head and the two delighted boys opened the box to cuddle their present.

Socks! I think the name was almost immediately bestowed upon the little fellow the moment we all saw his little white paws and he soon become a part of the household. We all enjoyed him. I remember having him sit on my lap as I studied for my public exams, but there were two people whose love for Socks transcended almost everything else: Ralph and my aunt, Mary. They adored him without absolutely any reservation whatsoever and when Socks passed away after sixteen-and-a-half years of faithful companionship, Aunty Mary was distraught. I remember writing a poem on the day I was informed of his death.

There was one person, though, who shunned Socks; he did not even want the little spaniel anywhere near him and that was Norman Papa. It was only after I had heard about his history with dogs that I was able to place his attitude towards Socks in much greater and more sympathetic perspective.

He had had to put down two big dogs of his own many years ago when they had been infected with the deadly rabies and he could no longer find himself getting attached to another canine companion. Apparently, I am told, that *Hollywoods* was a hive of animal activity in the early days of its existence mainly because of Nana Holly's love for animals.

When, due to changing circumstances, we had to relocate Mum-Mum and Socks to Mumbai, the little fellow became all the more protective of Mum-Mum in the big city; he enjoyed sitting by her side, in fact, at her very feet whenever he could. Aunty Mary was equally fond of him and treated him like a little child, taking him for long walks early every morning or late every afternoon.

Socks was encouraged to do the dingo-dango, where he would dance on his hind legs for a little treat. After our visits to Mumbai came to a close and the suitcases were lined up in readiness for yet another departure, Socks would go into a frenzied circle of barking and dancing. He did not want us to leave.

Like Socks, there are many felines and canines in Anglo-Indian houses, in India and abroad. No, I include them in this chapter not for any form of unique bond with the community, but because of a simple part of our humanity: a love of and a respect for animals.

Brother Ralph, with Socks.

Cousin Shelly Renaux with her pet, Brooke

Chapter 15

Putting the Pieces Together

"Do you speak English?" were David Ward's first words as he noticed an elderly lady approaching, from within the gate of a house that he seemed to be interested in. David and Hyacinth, in their quest for Hyacinth's own personal history, a quest I do believe that many first generation Anglo-Indian emigrants have embarked on in the last decade or so. They were visiting St Thomas Mount and were asking around tentatively, until some residents pointed them in the direction of houses that "had Anglo-Indians living there." Thus, the approach and the question!

Indignantly, the lady replied, "Of course, I do." The haughtiness in her voice took the gentleman by surprise.

David replied that they were actually looking for a house in which the *Younger* family might have been living in. Hyacinth, his wife, was the daughter of one Robina Younger, who had once been a resident of St Thomas Mount.

"I am a Younger," she haughtily responded and by this time, Hyacinth who had been poking around in the same vicinity, arrived by David's side. The conversation quite dramatically shifted gears and upon the questions and answers that were volleyed back and forth with the gate acting as a net, mutual realisation dawned and they all realised that she was Gwennie Gamble, a cousin of Hyacinth's Mum, Robina.

Hyacinth had at long last made the trip, not just to the land of her birth, but she was now standing on the very ground her mother once walked, putting the pieces together with a relative she met literally a few minutes ago. Remember, she was only four, when Denzil and Robina, with children Rodney and Hyacinth had set sail on the steamer from Bombay to Marseilles, from where they traversed France by train to board the ferry that would eventually take them from Calais to Folkstone in the United Kingdom.

The mutual inquisition now over, David and Hyacinth were invited in and they soon found themselves drinking tea and discussing family history. Those who had stayed behind had managed a rather serendipitous discovery of those who had gone away and found themselves in the rather fortunate position of putting the pieces of their separate and distinct lives together.

When I spoke to Hyacinth about this episode and she helped me with certain elements of this unexpected meeting, she emphasised on a rather interesting aspect of that reunion. Looking around, while she sipped tea and listened to tales long forgotten and stories retold yet another time, albeit to a new audience, Hyacinth could not help but notice that the "furniture, decor and feel of the house bore many similarities to the Fernandez HQ back in the UK." She was in a house she did not even know of until an hour or so ago and now she was sitting in it, feeling very much at home.

Of all the cousins I met during that August of 2009, Hyacinth is the one I am most in touch with and we keep in contact with the odd letter, email or phone call. She and David visited us around three years ago here in Zambia, where Hyacinth once again had the chance to reunite with her cousins, Pat and Jen, my father's sisters. All of us enjoyed their company as we took them on a true Zambian safari.

With the technologies we now have at our disposal and with air travel more accessible, I believe that reunions like the one I have just described are occurring all across the Anglo-Indian world, which only causes me to smile happily. Even if those scattered siblings of the diaspora never met each other ever again, at least their children and grandchildren are beginning to reunite and find added meaning to the lives they live and their very own Anglo-Indian jigsaw. At last, these reunions are putting the pieces together.

Nevertheless, I always feel a tinge of regret sometimes because there are some families out there who have not yet had the opportunity to build the bridges that would narrow the gap between themselves and their loved ones.

Hyacinth Ward, nee Fernandez, left in both pictures, top, with Pat Renaux and bottom, with Jennifer Thomas

Chapter 16

The Search

"It is only because you are an *Anglo-Indian* that you are embarking on all this family tree business. Look at me - I'm not worried about any family tree!" said Elizabeth, my wife, naughtily, to me one Saturday morning nearly six years ago.

I replied in kindred manner, "Of course, I need to put the pieces together. I obviously do have a French surname and I know now that I can trace my lineage back to Frederick Thomas Younger, who was Scottish. Don't you find it interesting?" I said, my eyes peeled to the computer as I continued searching the Internet for the many missing links in my personal history.

Armed with the knowledge that my grandparents were Agnes Gertrude Fernandez, Norman Charles White, Joseph Eugene Renaux and Flora Marjorie Younger, I decided to travel the Internet, and in a couple of instances, literally the world, to check my roots. I had that Alex Haley kind of feeling because I really did not know what I would unearth on this search.

I am yet to find any breakthrough on Fernandez side of the family. I know that Mum-Mum (Agnes) hailed from Tellicherry (Thalasherry, today), Kerala and in my curiosity, I learnt more colonial history than anything personal. Nevertheless, it was still knowledge enough to add value to my personal identity.

I checked all the genealogy websites available in abundance on the ubiquitous Internet and with a significant number of people asking questions of each other, leaving a trail of possible links and maybes, I did make significant headway with *White*. Norman was born to Archibald Aloysius Anthony White in Perambur, Madras in 1917 and Archibald himself was the son of a famous Irish doctor, who hobnobbed with the rich and famous of Madras in those days.

This search warranted a Facebook conversation and a subsequent telephone call over five years ago to Michael Ludgrove, presently in Bangalore and a second cousin once removed, a fact that I was blissfully unaware of until that phone call. Armed with our mutual knowledge, Michael and I realised that Samuel Charles White, the Irish doctor, had an estate in Madhavaram, Madras, called El Dorado and he, with his children and grandchildren, lived a privileged lifestyle. And one of those children decided to move to Arkonam, where I do believe he wanted to create an El Dorado of his own, but, as I keep informing you, dear reader, that is yet another story for yet another chapter.

Beyond Samuel White, I have not been able to go back any further, as information on his parentage does not seem quite forthcoming, but Michael - I am yet to meet him - believes that a photo that used to hang in *Hollywoods*, Arkonam, might help us even further. For now, the mystery continues, but I do know that Samuel Charles White's mortal remains were buried in St Roques cemetery, Royapuram!

On the Renaux side of the family, I hit better luck and, thanks again to the ubiquity of the Internet, managed to connect with a Gwen Middlecoat, who now lives in Harlow, UK. We have not managed to join the dots, but Gwen strongly believes that if we did a DNA test, it would prove our mutual genealogy.

On the Younger side of things I hit gold, and in doing so, made the maze I was already in, even murkier! Flora Marjorie Younger, my paternal grandmother was the second daughter of Frederick Thomas Younger, through his second marriage to Annie Wilkins. And, of course, with Flora's sister and brother-in-law still around at the time of my second visit to London, I was able to piece things together more clearly in the Younger corner of an amazing jigsaw. While Frederick had six children in his second marriage, he had ten in his first marriage, and while I am aware that his mortal remains were buried in St Thomas

Mount, Madras, I have been reliably informed that many of his children through his first marriage migrated to the UK, and Robina and Noreen were actually in touch with a couple of their step sisters. Talk about a colonial heritage.

Still on the Younger side of things, I came to make further connections and names like Gamble and Wilkins have since come into the picture! At the time of writing, I am well aware that further research will make the maze murkier and even more difficult to get out of, but that to me, is the fun of THE SEARCH!

At this very table, his neck in a brace, Uncle Denzil Fernandez regaled me with stories of a Madras he knew at a time when I was just about beginning the search.

With Norman Papa's cousin, Uncle Ted Scanlon and his wife Rose.

Chapter 17

Hollywoods

I remember a friend of mine telling me that he thought my family was being quite pretentious with the name that we had given our homestead. He had, in his ignorance, thought it had been named after that iconic celebrity town in Los Angeles. He could not have been further from the truth, for the origin of Hollywoods, Haffieldpet, Arkonam is a tale in itself and most worthy of a chapter on its own.

It is my opinion that Archibald Aloysius Anthony White wanted his own El Dorado, one modelled on his father's estate in Madhavaram, Madras. So I suppose, with his inheritance and blessings from his father, he travelled 70 kilometres North and arrived at a piece of virgin land where he decided to stake a claim and build his own house, a veritable mansion for Arkonam in that day and age.

The land he had acquired was a wooded region, half a kilometre away from the railway tracks, as the crow flies. He decided to raze the trees in the middle of woods and build his El Dorado there, but decided to name it Hollywoods.

No, he had no pretensions. His reasons were pure and simple. Archie Papa, as he was introduced to us in numerous stories told to us by Norman Papa, named his home after his wife, Gladys Smith, whose nickname was Holly! And since it was right in the middle of that vast wooded area, he called it Hollywoods.

Gladys Smith was Archie's second wife, and as my tale unfolds, you the reader, will understand why she had a heart of gold - and more.

Born in 1883 to Samuel Charles White, Archibald had married his first wife, Charlotte Cecilia Borgonha in 1909, but when Norman White, their first son was hardly ten years old, Charlotte passed away leaving behind a distraught Archibald with four young children, the youngest of whom was barely two. It was hardly moments after the funeral that Charlotte's mother spoke to Gladys - Charlotte's sister and herself recently widowed - to "marry Archie and look after the children."

Archie and Gladys would never have children of their own, but from the tales my grandfather, Norman, told me as we sat on the steps of Hollywoods and gazed into the night sky, Gladys was more than a mother to him and his siblings, Mildred, May and Geoffrey. In fact, even though I was barely four years old when she passed away, I do have a vague, but definite recollection of Gladys' body laid to rest in her room and how the entire colony seemed to fit into the room with the ayahs mourning in the loudest manner possible. I do not know if Norman Papa wept shamelessly on that day or not, but I do know that he held his step-mother in the highest esteem possible. In fact, even Mum-Mum, my grandmother, was extremely fond of and devoted to her mother-in-law.

Hollywoods was my home for twenty-one years, until I left it for good in the summer of 1999, and it gave me the best childhood any little boy could ask for. Now, as I write this personal tribute to Anglo-India, I feel the need to pay tribute to the woman who set the foundations for that childhood.

Holly really did have a heart of gold. She brought up her stepchildren with love, care and compassion. She was a teacher herself and instilled in them values that would make them all stand out in their own adult lives. I know Norman Papa was one of the most respected men around Arkonam town and he once told me that his mother - Gladys - gave him everything he needed to be the man he was. All I do know about Archibald White was that he knew Telugu fluently and was an adroit fencer. About Gladys, Aunty Holly as some called her, I learnt a lot and I still remember holding her by the hand - was she holding me, or I holding her, I cannot quite remember, but I do know that we were turning the corner from her bedroom to the dining room.

The town admired and respected Nana. They admired her because of "what she did for those children", including her grandchildren, Dawn (my Mum), Mary and Jean. They respected her for what she did for the town.

Haffieldpet, Arkonam, at the time, was just a colony with railway houses running parallel to the railway tracks and Hollywoods was the first house away from the colony, on the main road. Archibald had been a pioneer in that right, building his little tribute to his darling wife Holly in the middle of woods.

Slowly, though, other settlers came by, asking if "Holly would part with some of the land." While the rest of the family was apprehensive, Holly had no qualms at all. In fact, from the tales Norman Papa told me on those balmy September nights on the steps of Hollywoods, Nana - in the true spirit of humanity and humility - sold plots of land to the left, right and behind our house to everyone who asked, at very cheap prices. Apparently, she would say, after closing yet another ridiculous deal, "Son, they are also people like us, and they need to live." This one trait of hers was so enmeshed within her personality that she was defined by it within the community and the colony.

She looked after another man's children and she did not just look after them well. She brought them up brilliantly and she gave her name to a place I will always call home, no matter where I go or how affluent I become.

Thank you, Nana, Holly, for *Hollywoods*, the best home a child could ask for!

Great-grandma Holly, with little Alister and his brother, Mark,
Circa 1980. The R V Renaux family album

Hollywoods, home for nearly 20-21 years.
Artistic rendition – courtesy: R V Renaux

Chapter 18

Part of the Fabric

No book on Anglo-Indians would ever be complete without reference to a person who was, more often than not, an integral part of the household. And it is tribute to this individual's resilience, ability and dedication, that my mother, Dawn, sent me a message a few months ago: "Ruku passed away last night." I immediately responded with, "Is there anything I can do for the family?," to which she replied, "There is no family left. She did not have any children."

There was a small lump in my throat! I remember Ruku. Short, plump, forever smiling, forever talking, dependable, always looking out for me and my brother, Mark, especially for me, because I was her special one. In fact, even years later, when she came back to work with us as a maid, she always looked out for me even though I was now twelve years old. She said she would always do so because she was my first ayah!

Yes, assumedly like the Anglo-Indian, the ayah is a dying breed, but I hope my efforts will keep her memory alive, for almost every friend I knew had an ayah.

Ruku was my ayah. She cajoled me, she laughed with me, she put me to sleep. If I fell, she would check for any bruise; if I cried, she would put me on her strong shoulders and pat me gently. She would rock me on her lap, her saree spread out so that I could sleep all the more comfortably. She would talk to me in a language I had yet to understand; she often spoke reasonable broken-English to make me understand. She was by my side and I enjoyed her company. She played with me like one child would play with another.

I have vague memories of Ruku carrying me and cooking in the kitchen. In *Hollywoods* of that time, before four-burner stoves-cum-ovens became the norm, the kitchen was in an outhouse two metres behind the main house. In there, Ruku would put rice on the boil and she taught me how to blow - with something the name of which I forget - into the fire to keep it going. She would use a *chatty* - a black pot - to cook rice and fish. I was only five at the time, but I remember the smoke, the char and the room. It was black because of the amount of cooking Ruku did, but I still remember it to this very day. It was one of my favourite places, out of the house.

A little over a month ago, I had two teenagers who were doing a *braii*, Southern African for a BBQ, for a group of sixth graders camping out and these teenagers rushed to me saying their fire was dying out. Thank you, Ruku, you may have passed on, but to your credit, I blew life into that fire. I can picture us in that outhouse cooking on a fire with that *chatty* on the boil. I can remember you grinding out chutneys on a stone grinder, sitting on your haunches and laughing at me as I gazed, wondering.

Yes, the ayah made an Anglo-Indian household what it was, back in the day. She added her love, enthusiasm and devotion to children who were not her own and since this is, in many ways, a personal story, I cannot but add to this list, a woman who made my visits to Aunty Barbie's house in Little Mount, Madras, memorable: Govindamma.

I am now married, with two kids of my own, but whenever I go back to Little Mount to visit Aunty Barbie's daughter, Rosamund, Govindamma is still there. Aged over 80, she cheekily asks me how my naughty Dad is. Such is the devotion of the ayah.

Thus, with a lump in my throat, I end this chapter on a person who was, had been, and will always be part of the fabric called Alister Eugene Dominic Renaux.

An artistic illustration of a maid at work. Courtesy: Eugene D'cruz.

Chapter 19

A Scattered People

"They brought back many memories. We always had a meat safe with water under the legs, to keep the ants away. I remember the chest of drawers also. It was a must in every Anglo Indian home. Thank you for sending your writing to me." These were the words in an e-mail sent to me by Gwen Middlecoat, who now resides in Harlow, in the United Kingdom.

I got in touch with Gwen when both of us collided online while we were busy going through the maze of family history. You see, her mother was Daisy Elizabeth Renaux who married Percy Middlecoat, a railway driver on the North Western Railway. Gwen was born in 1933 in Rawalpindi, British India, now Pakistan and she lived in the country until 1989, after which she left for a holiday in the UK, where she eventually stayed on.

It was the first time I had ever come across an Anglo-Indian who originated from Pakistan, which sent my curious and analytical mind into overdrive.

Given that the entire Indian subcontinent - consisting of Bangladesh, Burma (Myanmar), India, Pakistan and Sri Lanka - was part of the British Raj until 1947, one must quite obviously accept the fact that there were British officials, businessmen and soldiers within this entire geographical region, called British India, which now consists of five entirely different countries. So, if you do meet someone of European ancestry from any of these countries, they too would be Anglo-Indian, thanks to their origins in British India.

If they were then born within these domiciles of the British Raj, they would either continue living there as my grandparents did or they might have moved out. So, yes, they might be Bangladeshi nationals, or citizens of Burma or Pakistan, but from an ethnic perspective, they are Anglo-Indians. In fact, the Bangladeshi Anglo-Indian population is only second to that of India's on the sub-continent. In Sri Lanka - once Ceylon - the teardrop island, with its Dutch, Portuguese and British influences, the mixed breed is officially recognised as the Burgher people, distant cousins perhaps to the Anglo-Indian. There is also a sizable community in Burma today. In Pakistan, the Anglo-Indians would probably number in the one thousands, should a census be taken.

My conversations with Gwen were always interesting, because they gave me the chance to look at the similarities in our lifestyles and yet, look at the differences that might have stemmed due to geographical distances. Gwen's maternal ancestors all hailed from Trichirapalli (then Trichinopoly) in South India, as did my paternal ones. Nevertheless, despite our efforts over the last five years, we haven't yet found the missing link. As I had said in an earlier chapter, Gwen believes that a DNA test would prove our family connections beyond the shadow of a doubt.

Gwen went on to tell me that she never mastered Urdu and how she would, in her role as Head teacher in Mianwali, Pakistan, communicate in a mixture of Urdu and Punjabi to parents who loved to hear her feeble, but valiant efforts. Gwen still has family in Pakistan and is in constant touch with them.

Yet, despite our many similarities - the meatsafe, the chest of drawers, the ballroom dances, the weddings, the dress and the demeanour - another aspect of Anglo-Indian life that fascinates me is the difference caused by geography, as stated earlier.

The Anglo-Indian is a scattered ethnic community. He is stateless, with no state of his own, but ironically spread out in many different Indian states. When I was growing up, I overheard many conversations about how the Andaman and Nicobar Islands might have been an

Anglo-Indian state, but it was never to be. Due to this immense geographic spread, I do believe that the Anglo-Indian from Calcutta might be - despite a common culture - very different from one let us say, in Madurai, Tamil Nadu. Which is why Gwen's experience of growing up in Pakistan would have been very different from my grandfather's experience of growing up in Tamil Nadu, even though her father and my grandfather had one thing in common: both were railway men.

The Anglo-Indian was certainly affected by geography and because of that geography he took on elements of his immediate surroundings so as to adapt and assimilate, while still retaining essential parts of his core identity.

For instance, many Anglo-Indians in the North of India might speak Hindi and prefer a cuisine based mostly on wheat, while those in the Southern states of Tamil Nadu and Kerala might speak the local languages of Tamil and Malayalam and prefer a cuisine in which rice is the staple food.

And this is what interests me the most: we are a scattered people in many ways, yet there are definitive thematic links in the way we cherish and treasure our mutual heritage, while, at the same time, having the adaptability and flexibility to integrate ourselves with the local mores, norms and attitudes of the various geographical states in which we grew up.

Chapter 20

A Sport Migrated

Many of the facts in this chapter are in the public domain, but while I state them, I would like to add my own perspective within the context and general theme of this book. The Anglo-Indian's contribution to Indian hockey has been appreciated to a degree relatively higher than his contributions elsewhere, but there is still much to be desired.

I do not know whether the reader might be aware that the definitive golden age of Indian hockey was between 1928 and 1956, and it might even be quite generously extended to 1960, when India secured the Silver medal at the Rome Olympics. A glance at the annals of Indian hockey would tell you so, for during that period of time the calibre of Indian hockey was literally a cut above the rest. To put it in a more modern context, one might coin the phrases - Boltesque or Phelpsian - to draw modern parallels to the level of hockey that India displayed at the Olympics during that period of time.

While the following facts are public knowledge, I do not know the extent to which the world, or for that matter, the present-day Anglo-Indian world, is aware of the level of Anglo-Indian influence and dominance within those hockey teams.

I remember Norman Papa, waxing lyrical about Dhyan Chand, who wielded his hockey stick with the aplomb of a magician and the grace of a conductor at the orchestra. He also offered me little snippets, which I can now place into much more mature and significant perspective. Dhyan Chand had a great supporting cast around him, as did the legendary Roop Singh, his brother. Between 1928 and 1947, these players had an Anglo-Indian support cast - at least seven or eight of the playing eleven on the field in the first three Olympics were all Anglo-Indian players.

The rugged British soldier - the private, not the officer - had imported hockey into India and very soon, the Anglo-Indian adopted it as a sport of his own - a sport that would, in many ways, define the Anglo-Indian identity. And, the Anglo-Indian would play his part on the national and the international stage, bringing Olympic glory to India, not once or twice, but on multiple occasions.

While the Anglo-Indian played his part in the halcyon days of Indian hockey, I dare suggest that he also played his part, albeit unintentionally, in the death of Indian hockey. Many blame cricket for hockey's demise, but I beg to differ. In today's world of "icon" players, opulence in cricket and the cash rich Indian Premier League, it is easy to lay the blame at cricket's doorstep as two of my Southern African colleagues recently did when, as sports enthusiasts we were discussing sport in general and the topic of India's dwindling powers as a once proud hockey nation.

Kapil Dev and his men won the World Cup only in 1983, a good three years after India had won its last Olympic medal, and while that did lead to cricket's rocketing emergence, one cannot be simplistic enough to say that cricket's growth in popularity led to hockey's diminishing esteem amongst the general Indian public.

Once again, ironic though it is, I intend for history to do the talking, for while well-documented records do exist, it is a pity that these records are not culturally significant enough for the general populace to understand the Anglo-Indian.

Let us go back to the D-word: diaspora. With the Independence movement gaining steam, a little before and most definitely after 1947 - and it is ironic that I write this the day after India's 69th Independence Day - the diaspora had begun and many Anglo-Indians were soon to be found in pockets of Western Australia, Melbourne in particular. Yes, and amongst this diaspora, were many talented hockey players.

73

Let us continue with history and check the record books now. When did Australia begin to emerge as a hockey playing nation? When did Australia begin to dominate the world as a hockey superpower? Look carefully, dear reader, and you might just make the connection with the Anglo-Indian diaspora. I do not intend to take any credentials away from the Australian nation for its sporting ethos and culture, for I have respect for its many national teams, as I do have for one of my favourite cricketers of all time, Steve Waugh. However, I also do intend to suggest that had the Anglo-Indian not imported hockey and his own talents into Australia in much the same way the ordinary British soldier did in India, Australia's passion for field hockey might not exist on the same plane or standard that it does today.

India's loss - Australia's gain. History speaks once again: a rather interesting tidbit to take away from a match in the 1960 Olympic games. The rival captains on the pitch that day were both Anglo-Indians. Did I say rival? How could it be remotely possible? Surely, if they came from the same community within India they should be on the same side of the pitch, not facing each other at the toss. But rival, they were: one Indian, one Australian; both Anglo-Indian.

Leslie Claudius faced off against Kevin Carton in an Olympic match in Melbourne 1960. The former had stayed behind, the latter had sailed away in 1948.

India would win two more Gold medals in hockey after that, the last of which came in Moscow, 1980. Australia, on the other hand, have placed in the top four in every Olympics since 1980 and have received medals in every Games between 1996 and 2012, becoming champions in Athens in 2004. The records alone speak for themselves.

Australia would benefit from the wealth of Anglo-Indian hockey that it imported post-1947. The Pearce family, interestingly, is Australia's most successful sporting family, having taken its talents to Australia from India, post-Independence. In fact, in the 1956 Olympics in Melbourne, when India played Australia there were five Anglo-Indians on the field that day: four for Australia, including three Pearce brothers; one for India, Leslie Claudius. However, that is not the purpose of this book. The purpose of this book, dear reader, is to point out that this resilient and talented community forged the sporting fortunes of two great nations, and yet, faces public ignorance worldwide.

Yet, it is part of history. A forgotten history. An unwritten history.

Today, hockey continues to thrive in colonies like Perambur, Trichy, Madurai, Podanur, Villupuram and Bangalore - all Anglo-Indian strongholds in the South of India. There are clubs in these colonies and they play fierce, competitive hockey amongst themselves in tournaments held on a regular basis. The most recent one was the Sinclair Family Tournament run by Adam Sinclair, who himself represented India at the Olympics in Athens, 2004.

George's Hockey Club. Photo courtesy: Karl Moses, far left.

Chapter 21

Assimilation

I remember meeting Roger McNamara in June 1997. He and I shared some wonderful conversations on poetry, literature and life. We discussed poets like Yeats, Keats, Wordsworth and Shelley, and amidst all those conversations a mutual respect and friendship grew and blossomed, so much so that when Elizabeth, Calvin and I decided to make a cross country tour of continental USA, we decided to meet up with this old friend in Chicago.

But when Roger first arrived at Loyola College, he was 'trending', to use a modern expression. The hostel students never seemed to be fascinated enough with this Anglo-Indian boy from Calcutta, and I soon found out the reason. Roger always walked in to the hostel dining hall armed with a spoon and fork!

Roger is old school, extremely old school, which is why he turned a raised eyebrow when he heard me use the word 'macha' when I addressed a friend. And like Roger, there are many Anglo-Indians, both in the North and the South of India who prefer eating with a spoon and fork, even amidst the bewildering glances from the people around them.

But, for some Anglo-Indians, it is a story of assimilation, especially for those who stayed behind. I can't ever remember Agnes White not using a spoon and fork when eating, but I was slowly growing up in a generation which was quietly acclimatising to and assimilating into the local way of life.

A Zimbabwean colleague once jokingly jibed that the only thing the British did not teach the Indians was how to use a spoon and fork. They did, actually; it is just that some of us prefer using our fingers, myself included. So yes, Anglo-Indian though I am, I do use my fingers to eat just about everything, with the exception of noodles and pasta! I guess it was assimilation by association.

And as we are on the topic, one of the favourite ways in which I like to eat is to have a 'thali' on a banana leaf. In fact, I take great pride in cooking a Malayalee feast for my Malayalee wife every *Onam*, a traditional harvest festival celebrated in Kerala, where meals are served on a banana leaf.

Roger was also surprised with my ability to speak Tamil, though I must say that I have never mastered the vernacular in Tamil Nadu and that my Tamil is highly accented. As I mentioned earlier, many Anglo-Indians in Tamil Nadu, my brother Mark included, have learnt to adapt and acclimatise by speaking the language as and when they need to. It is part of being an Anglo-Indian in a progressive India. I'd say acclimatisation by accommodation.

Aunty Barbie! My grandaunt was always impeccably dressed every Sunday as she walked to church. Dressed in her Sunday best, with her hat on her head and a cane in her hand, she would walk to the Little Mount church, quite regal in her bearing. She would never acclimatise; she couldn't! She was born long before India gained Independence and her colonial heritage was part and parcel of her demeanour.

I though, could acclimatise, if I wanted to - and I wanted to.

I remember a maid asking me in my early days in Zambia, "*Bwana*, why are you wearing a *chitenge*? Only women wear it here in Zambia." I had to explain that I was not wearing a chitenge, but a *lungi* instead! None of my brothers wears one, though Dad used to, once upon a time. I wear it almost every day once I get back home from work. I know a few uncles who do and many who don't. The lungi is a wrap-around piece of cloth worn by many men in South India and I like the comfort I get by wrapping it around my waist. This time it wasn't acclimatisation by association or accommodation; it was acclimatisation by choice.

Yes, I do believe that the Anglo-Indian story is one of acclimatisation, which is why our food is unique. We took elements of British cuisine and blended it with elements of Indian food to come up with an Anglo-Indian palate. The ability to adapt and acclimatise to both these cultures is what makes our heritage a unique and historical one.

Dad wearing a lungi and putting his twins to sleep - 1985
The R V Renaux family album

Chapter 22

Coming Together

Mum-Mum wasn't too well a summer before I left Arkonam for good. I remember feeding her soup one evening, when quite unannounced, in walked Aunty Jenny Jeremiah to check up on the 'patient'. Our next-door neighbour, Aunty Jenny would walk in every evening to check up on Mum-Mum. So would Aunty Buddy Marshall, who lived just behind Aunty Jenny's house.

It was late one night when I heard a knocking on the door, and upon opening the trellised door, I recognised Mary Hussey's face and voice, "Daddy's dead." Mum immediately went over to the Hussey's to offer assistance.

Aunty Bridget Fernandez passed away a few days after my brother Mark's wedding. Mum and Dad were in Chennai at the time and they didn't hesitate to book a car so that they could travel to Arkonam to be there at her funeral.

When Aunty Jean Douyere passed away in the summer of 2005, Mark and I didn't blink an eyelid as we travelled from Chennai to Arkonam on motor-bike to represent our Mum and Aunty Mary - who always visited the Douyeres whenever she came from Bombay to Arkonam.

I remember bumping into Troydon Scurville at Chennai Central Railway station one afternoon. His words chilled me, "Alister, Aunty Sybil Fenwick passed away early this morning." I was stunned. Only the previous Sunday I had sat just outside the Fenwick's house and had a drink with Gene and Dean Fenwick. Gene was impassive at her funeral, just staring at her coffin being lowered into the ground. Two weekends later as we sat on the steps of his house, a glass of whiskey in our hands, Gene broke down and wept. I quietly told him it was okay.

The list is endless. Jerry Moses spent an entire night with me as we kept vigil over Norman Papa's body as it was laid out that December night in Arkonam.

The Douyeres assisted Mum when I had to go into hospital for an emergency appendix operation when I was around thirteen.

I do not know how many of my friends in Arkonam remember, but I do. We watched the 1999 World Cup cricket final in the Sladen's house, devouring turtle soup and meat as we watched Australia annihilate Pakistan.

In other words, the community always, and I have to repeat the word always, came together.

I personally saw it in the helpfulness of a Felicity Saldanha, Phillip Jeremiah, Barry Wlison, Phillip Marshall or a Bruce Dickson. I saw it in Arkonam and in Trichy, a city where I spent quite a few summers. Both are railway communities and in both of them I saw that sense of coming together as one in the people themselves: simple and always ready to give.

That is the Anglo-Indian way. To come together and give; and that is what makes us unique as a community.

Photo Courtesy: Eugene D'Cruz
This photograph is emblematic of the spirit of
coming together within the community.

Chapter 23

Identity Revisited

In the course of writing this book, I was in constant contact with Hyacinth, who had, of course, sailed away all those years ago in 1963 only to set eyes on India in 2010. Hyacinth gave me a few insights which, I believe, are critical to the many underlying themes within this book.

After reading the bulk of my manuscript, Hyacinth made relevant comments which warrant another chapter where I once again place personal perspective against the backdrop of Anglo-Indian culture at large.

While the Anglo-Indian might have sailed away either to Australia, England or Canada, like his hockey, he took other parts of Anglo-India with him. As Hyacinth says in an earlier chapter, sitting in Gwennie Gamble's house in St Thomas Mount reminded her so much of her early days in "Fernandez HQ" in London.

Yes, the Anglo-Indian took his way of life, his culture and his cuisine as he sailed away to the corners of the Commonwealth in the hope of a better future, especially for his young children.

In essence, Anglo-India continued to thrive, silently in little homes dotted across the aforementioned countries. Hyacinth tells me that Jim Reeves was often heard crooning through the stereo in Fernandez HQ. Uncle Denzil loved his Country and Western music and his three children grew up listening to it. So in pockets of Australia, the UK and Canada, or wherever in the world he might be found, the Anglo-Indian carried his music with him. He might have sailed away, but the "music in his heart he bore" so that one day, he could play it all the more.

Hyacinth again tells me that while the word "bloody" might still have the connotations of a swearword in the UK, she and her family still use the word in its Anglo-Indian sense - and essence. Likewise, I am sure that many Anglo-Indian families scattered across the globe today do have the occasional coconut rice and ball curry on a Sunday or any other special occasion. The Anglo-Indian, in my opinion, continued living his life and retaining his culture. No, the culture is not dying out; in fact, it never has been fading away, which brings me to my next line of reasoning.

A fortnight from today, there will be an Anglo-Indian reunion dance in Melbourne for the Anglo-Indians from Arkonam, a charity Dinner Dance being held to assist the less fortunate Anglo-Indians from the colony. These dinner dances have been a regular feature over the last two decades and have, as such, opened up articles on the revival of Anglo-Indian culture.

Revival? I do not think so. A continuation, as this chapter suggests, would be a better word, a stronger and more vibrant continuation. You see, dear reader, when the Anglo-Indian left the shores of India, the maximum amount he could carry in his pocket was the measly sum of $7, which, even if one accounts for inflation, was relatively little in those days. He had to fend for himself and his young family. He quietly continued his traditions in his kitchen, living room and on the sports field.

Today, though, his children are relatively more affluent than he was when he started out as an immigrant and these children are either old enough to remember the idyllic and halcyon days in their colonies or too young to know their rich and varied heritage. So, with a more affluent background mingled with nostalgia in one generation and curiosity in the other, the Anglo-Indian in the Commonwealth is not in the process of rediscovering a culture; he is in the process of reaffirming a culture that he can now proudly call his own.

Yes, the identity crisis of the late 1800s and early 1900s is over. The Anglo-Indian is proud of who he is and he is not afraid to tell the world where he comes from and where he intends to go. He is now comfortable with his identity because he has forged it himself: he may be Australian or Canadian, Indian or British - those might be his nationalities - but in essence he is Anglo-Indian - that is his true identity.

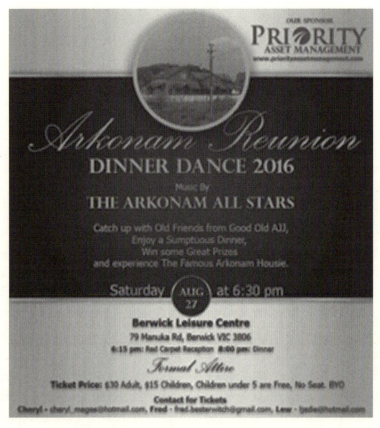

The invitation says it all. Expect ballroom
dancing in full flow at one of these!

Chapter 24

Ency Whyte

When Norman Charles White died in December 1993, I got the news over the phone through Aunty Rosamund, when I was staying at a friend's place because my board exams were just about six months away. It was six-forty-five in the morning and I was called away from my breakfast table to answer the phone. I remember replying, "Oh, bloody hell!" the first time I swore not at, but to a family member.

I remember arriving at school and Mark, my brother, met me to say, "Papa is in a really bad condition." Mark had travelled on the five o'clock train early that morning and had not heard the news yet - no mobile phones in 1993. I bluntly told him, "Norman Papa is dead," on the grounds of St Bede's Anglo-Indian Higher Secondary School. I told him to go home promptly and that I would follow immediately after writing my first Physics mock exam. That was the least I could do.

I wrote that exam with tears smeared all over my face. I wanted to go home, but I sat for three hours writing that exam because I knew that was what Norman Papa would have wanted me to do. At twelve-thirty that afternoon I called my hosts - Mum's friends, the Nanus, to say I was taking the train to Arkonam. I do not remember much of the train ride, but I do remember walking up the roads lining the railway colony to our house just outside of it, on Mosur Road, Arkonam.

His body was laid out in the living room of *Hollywoods* and visitors - that Anglo-Indian community - kept coming and going in droves. There were many outside of the community who came to pay their respects.

I was astounded at the wealth of affection for a man I always adored. To me, Norman Charles White was the greatest person in the world.

I vividly remember when Aunty Mary - his eldest daughter - having just flown in from Mumbai walked into the house sobbing. I was standing on the steps of Hollywoods with Charmayne Fernandez telling her that my Aunty would go ballistic, which she did. Aunty Mary loved her father for all he did for her. Norman Papa used to put her on his lap as he read to her the Jim Corbett stories. She was distraught to have lost a man dear to her heart; as was Mum!

Norman Papa! I remember reading a lesson at his funeral. I had to. He was my mentor, the man who took me on his bicycle, the man who made me overcome many fears, the man who carried me on his shoulders when I was a mere child. He was a strong man and stocky too. He taught me so much in the seventeen years that I knew him.

I hated funerals back then. In fact, when Aunty Barbie had died two years earlier, I did not even enter the cemetery, not wanting to hear or see the wails and the tears. At Norman Papa's funeral, I remember standing next to Mum-Mum and lifting her by the shoulders, stoic in my demeanour as I quietly told her to let go. The boy had become a man. No one saw my emotions that day, but when I went back home and sat on my bed that night, I looked into the mirror and at a photograph of Norman Papa, and wept unabashedly.

As a tribute to the man, his son-in-law, Dad, actually begged for leave at his workplace in Muscat, Oman, so that he could be with Mum at the funeral. I recall him saying, "The Director kept saying, 'Robert, it is only your father-in-law, not your father!'" But, Dad was adamant and made it just in time for the funeral, not because it was only his father-in-law, but because it was definitely his father-in-law.

A favourite story that I am quite keen on is the one told to me by Eugene D'cruz, a gentleman a few years younger than both my grandparents. Apparently, N C White and J E Renaux would finish off an entire basket of *vadas* - a spicy South Indian snack - that they would purchase from a vendor who used to pass by the railway shed. They could eat. And wrestle!

According to Uncle Eugene, the entire shed at AJJ (Arkonam Joint Junction) would wait for the wrestling matches between my two grandfathers. Both strong, both fit, both muscular; one tall and lean at 6 feet 6 inches, the other short and stocky at 5 feet 4 inches. Apparently, there was never a winner as they both tried to prise each other off the ground. In fact, the onlooking railwaymen would try to poke them in the ribs or pinch them on their bottoms to see if one would relent over the other. They never did; they never would. They were proud men; they were railwaymen; they were my grandfathers.

Norman White was a legend in Arkonam. He read and served at morning mass; he cycled to and from the market buying anything needed for the house; he let his little grandchildren sit on his tummy as he lay on the steps of *Hollywoods* and regaled them with stories. He was almost always the first person to be called when there was a death in the community. He was there to wash the dead body and to stay with the family, often through the night and until the next day, when he would literally jump into the grave to help lower the casket. He was always there.

The children giggled with him, not at him; the teenagers enjoyed the jokes and banter he shared with them; the adults relied on him and the elderly knew he would do odd jobs for them that they could no longer do. He was Mr Dependable.

That was until the last few years of his life, which, even to this very day, are inexplicable to me. How could that stocky, powerful and strong man succumb to something like depression I would never know - or fathom. Now, when I look back, it eats at me! I was a teenager at that time, powerless then. Only if I had the knowledge, wisdom and advice I now dole out to nervous teenagers, I might have helped, but back then, I was a nervous teenager myself. I just stood and sat and watched as the most dominant force in my life was withering away before my eyes. I had to get used to seeing him becoming a feeble man; an ironic shadow of his former self.

If I love the English language today, it is because of him. He even taught me how to parse a sentence! If I ask my wife to read my writing today and comment on it, it is because he always had Agnes White vet his work before he sent it to the magazines. He read and he wrote. I write and I read. His single-most important trait was his helpfulness and I can confidently say that he passed on that quality to each one of his grandchildren who had the pleasure to know him.

That is why I write, often not under my own name, but that of Ency Whyte.

Norman Charles White with a grinning Alister Renaux on his lap, while Agnes Gertrude White (Mum-Mum) with a pensive Mark on hers.
R V Renaux family album.

Singing in the Kitchen

There are recipes galore on the Internet and it would seem pointless repeating them here, but the recipes I am adding to this book are my own, made for family, friends and neighbours with a few personal tweaks here and there.

Moreover, I title this *Singing in the Kitchen* because I personally love listening to music, especially Country and Western, when prepping and cooking. It reminds me so much of my days in *Hollywoods*. The stew, for instance, was prepared while listening to two of my favourite classics, Kenny Rogers' *Lucille* and *Coward of the County*.

Dumpling Stew Vegetarian Style

Recently, we had a vegetarian couple over for dinner and I wanted to cook something Anglo-Indian. A tough task given that much of our cuisine is non-vegetarian. Nevertheless, the dish was a success! I made the same dish with beef two days later and Calvin wanted thirds! Here it is:

Ingredients

Coconut cream - 2 cups
Flour - 6 tablespoons
Chillies - 2 (depending on how hot you want it)
Ginger - 1 inch piece
Garlic - 1 clove
Bay leaf - 2
Carrots - 2
Beans - 200 gms
Cauliflower - 1 small sized
Peas - 100 gms
Potato - 2 medium sized ones
Peppercorns - 5 or 6
Cinnamon - 1 stick

Cloves - 4 or 5
Turmeric - a pinch

For the dumplings:
Knead 3 tablespoons of the household flour in a bowl with a dash of salt. Once it is firm, roll the dough flat and make flat little triangles. Keep aside.
For the stew:
Boil the vegetables in coconut cream, a pinch of turmeric and a cup of water for five minutes. Pour in the bay leaf, ginger, garlic, peppercorns, cinnamon and cloves and boil for another five minutes. Add the two slit chillies now for some heat, and toss in the triangular-shaped dumplings. After three more minutes, sift in the remaining tablespoon of flour for added thickness. Enjoy with roti, naan or bread!

Mum-Mum's Homemade Ginger Wine

I have made this twice at Christmas time. It is something I believe is authentically Anglo-Indian.

Ingredients:

600 gms ginger
6 bottles of water
18 limes
4-and-a-half pounds of sugar
10 cloves
3 nutmegs
4-5 sticks of cinnamon

Method: Burn half the quantity of sugar. Wash the ginger and dry it out. Then, slice the ginger fine.
Next, add the water, sliced ginger, spices, and the remaining sugar and boil it for an hour. Then, add the lime juice and let it bubble boil.

Let it stand for a day or two. Next, strain it through muslin cloth and into an earthen jar. Will be ready for use in 2 or 3 weeks.

Pepperwater

Show me an Anglo-Indian who does not like pepperwater! However, my pepperwater is a slight hybrid like myself and I include it because I often share it with my Pakistani and Mauritian neighbours, who enjoy it as a drink or with boiled rice.

Ingredients:

Tomatoes - 4 medium sized
Tamarind paste - One small ball

To crush:
Two cloves garlic
Ginger - 1 inch piece
Cumin seeds - a tablespoon
Peppercorns - one tablespoon
Green chillies - Two
For the seasoning:
Onion - one medium sized
Mustard - a teaspoon
Two sprigs of curry leaves
Dry red chillies
A generous bunch of fresh green coriander leaves
A teaspoon Rasam powder - optional - and only if you want a more South Indian rather than Anglo-Indian taste.

Method:
Boil tomatoes to a nice pulp while crushing the second group of ingredients to a coarse paste in a mortar and pestle. Add a litre of water and bring to bubble boil. If you want a more South Indian taste, add rasam powder and let it simmer. Add salt to taste.

While it simmers, heat oil in a pan and when it is hot, add the ingredients listed for seasoning or tempering.

Throw this seasoning mixture into the simmering pepperwater or throw the pepperwater into the simmering mixture. It is bound to sizzle, either way.

Turn off the stove. Throw in a generous bunch of fresh green coriander and cover. Let it stand for ten minutes.

Serve hot with rice, dal mash and fried fish. Alternately, drink it as a nice, hot soup. Ideal on a rainy day or when you have a bad cold.

The Rationale Behind this Book

History has been unfair to Anglo-Indians - that is the premise of this book. Its purpose is to show the world the true imprint of the Anglo-Indian community on the history of India by outlining its culture, identity and sense of community through a personal retelling of the author's own story by recounting memories that are bound to stimulate notes of nostalgia within the community and provide an interesting insight of what it means to be Anglo-Indian to those who are unaware of this uniquely mixed breed. It is an Anglo-Indian story with a personal flavour; an Anglo-Indian biography seen through an autobiographical lens.

St Theresa's Church, Haffieldpet, Arkonam.
Illustration: courtesy, Eugene D'cruz

27709096R00065